I
Lack
Patience

Finding Calm In A Chaotic World.

I Lack Patience

Finding Calm In A Chaotic World.

S.K. Luke

"Patience is bitter, but its fruit is sweet." — Jean Jacques Rousseau

Copyright
I Lack Patience
S.K. Luke

First Edition, 2025
© S.K. Luke, 2025. All rights reserved.

No part of this publication may be reproduced, stored in a retrieval system, or transmitted in any form or by any means—electronic, mechanical, photocopying, recording, or otherwise—without the author's or publisher's prior written permission.

Requests for permission or inquiries should be directed to the author.

IBSN: 978-93-342-8523-9

"To my wife, who always saw my potential, and for her patience that carried me when I needed it most."

Also, by S.K Luke

Fictional

Milo the Cat – A Day Out
Villy the Vulture
Jeron and John – High and Fly
Ben the Bear
Who's in the ATTIC
Binny n Bonny
Bella's Boat Escapade
Tales of the Mochi Wala – The Cobbler
Silence Whispers

Non-Fictional

Decoding Maturity
Navigating the Grey

Contents

1. **Impatience Epidemic** – *Struggle With Patience*   1

    Many Faces of Impatience   5
    Impatience – A Daily Impulse   9
    Living in the Fast Lane   12
    The Continuum Framework   14
    The Impatience-To-Patience Continuum Framework   17
    The Power of Gradual Shifts   20
    Applying the Continuum Concept   21
    Practical Exercise: The Impatience-to-Patience Shift   23

2. **Impatient Me** – *Understanding My Triggers*   27

    Pattern Of Impatience   29
    The Common Triggers Of Impatience   30
    Shaping Patience's Path   33
    Patience In Adversity   35
    Psychological Impact - The Hidden Mental Toll   37
    Reframing Impatience - Shifting Perspective   41
    Patience Is A Practise, Not A Trait   44

3. **Why We Rush** – *Unpacking The Roots*   49

    Patience Puzzles – Triggers and Influences   50
    The Perfect Trap   52
    The Fallout – How Impatience Hits Home   55
    Charting Impatience's Sparks   55
    Rooting Out Impatience   61

4. Cost of Impatience – *How Frustration Affects My Life*   67

    The Personal Price – When Impatience Robs Me of Peace   68

    The Hidden Toll – Stunting Growth and Well-Being   71

    The Patience Pyramid   72

    The Modern Dilemma of Impatience   74

    Measuring the Cost – Are You Impatient? A Quick Check   77

5. Social Factors – *A Patience Trap*   83

    Rushing to Results – Workplace Success   85

    The Ticking Clock – Relationship Dynamics   88

    Impatience in Everyday Life   90

    The Social Pulse   92

    The Social Getaway – The Patience Toolbox   95

6. Mindset Shift – *Reframing Our Lenses*   101

    A Mindful Turn   102

    The Power of Small Shifts   103

    Self-Compassion – Being Kind to Ourselves   104

    Changing Our Perspective on Time   105

    Mind Over Matter   106

    Waiting vs Waiting Patiently   108

    Mindset vs. Reaction   111

    Understanding Growth Mindset   113

    Reframing Patience as a Strength   114

    The Science Behind Patience and Success   116

7. A World in A Hurry – *A New Normal*   119

    The Erosion of Patience in Modern Society   121
    Manifestations Of Patience   131
    Starved World – The Price Of Playing With Patience   132

8. Accept What We Can't Control – *A Reflection*   135

    Macro Patience and Micro Controls   136
    Navigating Fixed Structures   138
    Embracing Life's Uncertainty   140
    Active and Inactive Patience   141
    Social Dynamics: Accepting Others' Choices   143

9. Leadership In An Impatient World   147

    The Power of Patience – A Leadership Imperative   149
    How Most Leaders Thrive In an Impatient World   151
    Applying "Expectancy Theory" in Leadership   154
    Consistently Reliable, Occasionally Extraordinary   157

10. Cultivating Patience   161

    Emotional Intelligence And Self Awareness   162
    Meditation and Mindfulness – Reframing Perspective   164
    Time Management and Prioritisation   165
    The 5-Step Model   170

Activities   175

Selective Readings   199

Preface

In the wilds of Kenya, the *Maasai tribe,* famed for their lion-hunting prowess, teaches us an extraordinary lesson in patience. It is said that lions retreat when they see the Maasai, recognising their distinct stance, posture, or long stride. This speaks volumes about the Maasai's presence in nature. From a young age, they are taught to move with purpose and confidence, understanding that survival is not about rushing in but about timing and awareness. Their patience is not passive—*a quiet, disciplined strength that allows them to stay still and composed, even in the face of danger.* The Maasai know true power lies in recognising when to act and when to wait. It's a wisdom that applies as much to our personal and professional lives as to the savannah. Sometimes, the most significant victories come not from rushing but from knowing the right moment to strike.

Let's be honest—*patience isn't my strongest suit*. It has been the root of many struggles in my work and personal life, and I know I am not alone. I am the kind of person who wants everything done yesterday—*fast results, quick wins, and no time to waste*. That drive can feel empowering, but it often comes at a cost. You will know what I mean if you thrive on that same urgency.

The battle between patience and success is real. Impatience can be the fuel that drives us forward—you think, *"If I don't move quickly, I will fall behind."* But here's the kicker: impatience and success don't always go hand in hand. Rushing can lead to mistakes, missed opportunities, and burnout. I've learned that slowing down, stepping back, and embracing patience sometimes lead to far better outcomes. *It's a journey—a lesson in growth.*

Think of it this way: your mind is like a car engine. You can push it to the max and go fast, but you will burn out if you do not let it cool down. Impatience pushes you to perform, but without breaks, it leaves you stuck in the emotional equivalent of traffic jams. I have learned (often too late) that practising patience is not about slowing down but avoiding a crash.

Patience has been the quiet force behind some of the most outstanding achievements throughout history. Napoleon's haste cost him in Russia, while Nelson Mandela's patient endurance over 27 years of imprisonment changed a nation. Even modern examples like *Elon Musk*—who faced failure after failure with SpaceX before reaching success—or *Thomas Edison*, who persevered through countless lightbulb prototypes, show that persistence and patience often win the day.

Personally, impatience has been my constant companion. It has driven me forward but also pulled me off course. As a *perfectionist*, I expect tasks to be done yesterday, often pushing my team too hard to keep up. Over time, I have realised that patience is not just a virtue but a crucial part of success. Without it, we risk burnout, strained relationships, and lost opportunities. Ironically, it is impatience that slows us down in the long run.

Stephen Covey's words, *"The key is not to prioritise what is on your schedule, but to schedule your priorities,"* have stuck with me. I often miss what is most important in my rush to finish things. Patience is not about waiting—thinking, planning, and acting purposefully. It holds

Preface

relationships together, helps you focus on what matters, and clarifies chaos. Without it, life becomes a whirlwind.

So, where does impatience hit you *hardest? At work? At home?* Maybe it is the little things—waiting in line, a slow internet connection. We all face it. The key is recognising these moments and using them as opportunities to reflect. As Jean Jacques said, *"Patience is bitter, but its fruit is sweet."* Those challenging moments of waiting often lead to the most rewarding outcomes.However, why is impatience so prevalent? Is it something we are born with, or does it come from our fast-paced environment?

For many of us, impatience is a product of our world—social media, instant messaging, and constant notifications—all designed to make us seek instant gratification. On top of this, the pressures from work and personal life don't help. Younger generations often feel driven by ambition, while older generations may have come to value the journey, not just the destination. Yet, the insecurity of life usually takes the driver's seat, pushing us toward impatience. We struggle with a healthy relationship with time, and this disconnect prevents patience from flourishing, allowing impatience to take root.

Professions like finance or healthcare demand quick decisions, while others, like art or research, require a reflective pace. Patience is not a "one-size-fits-all" quality—it is about knowing when to act fast and when to take your time.

Here is the good news: *Patience is a skill, and skills can be learned.* You do not have to erase impatience—it is part of being human. However, you can manage it, recognise its triggers, and use it as a tool for growth. It takes awareness, practice, and reflection.

I Lack Patience

My goal here is to invite you on a journey of *self-awareness*. Together, we will explore ways to manage impatience, understand its roots, and transform it into something positive. The process will not be simple, but it will be worth it. Through practical exercises, insights, and lessons from history, you will see how patience can fuel personal growth and lead to lasting success.

Ultimately, this journey is about learning to move with purpose, like the *Maasai*—knowing when to act and when to wait. Like *Edison*, whose persistence lit up the world, you will find that the slow and steady path is sometimes the most powerful.

How Is The Book Structured?

Lack Patience explores why impatience dominates our lives and how cultivating patience can lead to lasting success. Through ten chapters, I share personal reflections, historical lessons, and actionable strategies to build patience and transform your approach to life.

1. **The Impatience Epidemic** - This chapter explores how modern life, fuelled by *instant gratification* and *technology*, fosters impatience. I introduce the *Impatience-to-Patience Continuum*, a concept that illustrates the spectrum of impatience and patience, and offer *mindfulness exercises* to recognise impatience in everyday frustrations.

2. **The Impatient Self** - I delve into my triggers—*stress* and *perfectionism*—and help readers identify their impatience triggers. Through *mindful reflection*, I encourage readers to regain composure and make more thoughtful decisions.

3. **Roots of Impatience** - Impatience stems from *various societal pressures* and ingrained habits. For instance, there is pressure to meet deadlines at work, or the habit of expecting immediate responses in communication. I highlight historical examples, like the *Crimean War*, to help readers spot their triggers and transform impatience into *personal growth*.

4. **Costs of Impatience** - This chapter highlights the consequences of impatience—*burnout*, *strained relationships*, and poor decisions. The *Patience Pyramid* provides a roadmap to replace short-term haste with lasting patience, underlining the issue's urgency.

5. **Social Influences** - I address how societal pressures amplify impatience, including workplace demands and social expectations. The

Patience Toolbox offers tools like *empathy* and *communication skills* to foster patience in relationships.

6. **Mindset Transformation** - Patience is an *active skill*. Inspired by *Stephen Covey's* focus on prioritising, I encourage a *growth mindset* that turns challenges into opportunities and builds *resilience*.

7. **A Culture of Haste** - This chapter examines how *technology* and *social norms* erode patience. I discuss how our brains chase instant rewards and advocate for patience to improve *long-term well-being*.

8. **Accepting the Uncontrollable** - I reflect on the profound importance of accepting what's beyond our control. Inspired by *Nelson Mandela*, I show how *letting go* fosters stronger relationships and inner peace, offering the audience a sense of tranquility.

9. **Leadership and Patience** - Patience is key to effective leadership. I explore how leaders can balance *short-term pressures* with long-term vision, drawing inspiration from *Elon Musk's perseverance*.

10. **Cultivating Patience** - The final chapter offers practical tools—*meditation, emotional intelligence*, and *time management*—to help you develop patience in everyday life. My *5-Step Model* guides readers to manage impatience triggers.

Finally, I will provide *activities* that might help you build personal patience alongside *resources* like *books*, *online courses*, and *workshops* for further growth. *I Lack Patience* invites readers to reflect on their impatience, guided by *Aristotle's wisdom* that patience yields "sweet fruit" and the Maasai's purposeful pacing.

1.

IMPATIENCE EPIDEMIC – *Struggle With Patience*

"One minute of patience, ten years of peace." - Greek Proverb

In 1983, during an agitated moment in the Cold War, Soviet officer Stanislav Petrov made a decision that possibly *saved the world*. The Oko early warning system had signalled an incoming missile strike from the United States. The official protocol was clear—*retaliate*. But Petrov *paused*. He suspected a *malfunction* and, despite the enormous pressure, he *waited*. He sought *confirmation*, refusing to act on fear alone. In doing so, he demonstrated extraordinary *patience*, *maturity*, and *rational judgment*. He didn't panic or allow emotion to cloud his thinking. His calm, measured response stands as a powerful example of what it means to keep one's *head steady* under the most extreme circumstances.

I often reflect on this story, particularly when I find myself grappling with *impatience*. Petrov's restraint reminds me that slowing down, taking stock, and resisting the urge to act hastily is not weakness—it's a deliberate form of *strength*. In a world that idolises speed and instant reaction, *patience* is nothing short of *revolutionary*.

I Lack Patience

Have you ever been so immersed in something like writing that the thought of stepping away feels like a betrayal? That's precisely how I felt after completing my latest book, *Navigating the Grey*. The writing process was a marathon—*exhilarating*, *exhausting*, utterly *consuming*. I'd promised myself a proper rest once it was finished. A time to *breathe*, to let my mind *wander* without the weight of deadlines or word counts.

But the moment I set the manuscript aside, my mind spun into overdrive: *What's next? What should I be focusing on now?* Even while pottering about the kitchen, stirring soup, or slumping on the sofa with a cuppa, I couldn't shake a lingering *guilt*—as though doing nothing was a waste of time.

And perhaps that's where Petrov's story speaks to me most. Sometimes the bravest, wisest thing we can do is *wait*. To be *still*. Trust that there is still movement in the quiet, in the absence of doing. The truth is, I've never had a healthy relationship with *time*. I want everything done *now* perfectly, with no delays—not just for me, but for my team, my department, and everyone relying on me.

One evening, my wife found me hunched over my laptop, deep in research for a new project. I had promised her, hours earlier, that I'd take a proper break—no faffing with work, no "just five more minutes." She leaned against the doorway, arms folded, and with a cheeky grin said, "You've got *no patience*, have you? You were meant to be on a break." It was light-hearted, but it struck home like a quiet thunderclap. She was *right*. *Patience* has never been my strong suit—I barrel through tasks, chase the next milestone, and find sitting still feels like *wading through treacle*.

IMPATIENCE EPIDEMIC – *Struggle With Patience*

Her words lingered, nudging me into *self-reflection*. It wasn't just about the book or the break. It was a thread running through my life—this restless *impatience* that seems to surface in so many ways. The more I paid attention, the more I noticed how impatience had infiltrated my daily routine. I rushed through tasks, checked the time obsessively, sought instant results, and constantly felt like I wasn't doing enough.

Over time, I realised that impatience wasn't just an occasional nuisance but a key driver behind stress, *overwhelm*, and that persistent sense of *dissatisfaction*. Confronting it became not only necessary but transformative. It's inspiring to know that embracing patience can transform our lives and help us find a sense of peace and satisfaction.

"Patience is not the ability to wait, but the ability to keep a good attitude while waiting." This quote, often attributed to *Immanuel Kant*, challenges our typical view of patience. In his *Critique of Practical Reason* (1788), Kant explores how *reason* governs our actions, especially in times of difficulty or uncertainty. He argues that true moral strength doesn't lie in merely enduring delays but in maintaining a composed and thoughtful mindset.

For Kant, *patience* is an *active virtue*—a conscious decision to remain calm, resilient, and grounded, even when the world insists we rush. It's not about how long we wait, but *how* we wait. The *quality* of our patience is revealed through our *attitude* during those moments. Think of the times you've waited for a promotion, a life-changing decision, or navigated through a period of uncertainty. What defined the experience was not the duration, but your *mental state* while waiting.

In today's culture of *instant gratification*, the virtue of patience is often overlooked. Yet Kant's perspective reminds us that patience is about *strength*, *self-discipline*, and the *wisdom* to understand that timing, not speed, is usually the key to success. Considering Kant's perspective and how it can guide our daily lives is intellectually stimulating.

We live in a world that moves at breakneck speed—relentlessly pushing us to *do more*, *achieve more*, be *constantly on*. But what if the real solution lies in *slowing down*? In embracing *stillness*, *reflection*, and *deliberate calm*? This shift in thinking has inspired my next project—exploring how we can live more *patiently*, with greater *awareness*, and less *urgency*. Because ultimately, *self-awareness* forms the foundation of personal growth and genuine fulfilment. It's empowering to know that by cultivating self-awareness, we can take control of our personal growth and find true fulfilment.

Consider the Challenger disaster in 1986—a tragic example of how *impatience* can have devastating consequences. Engineers raised concerns about the spacecraft's O-ring seals in cold temperatures, which were overruled in the rush to meet the launch schedule. The result was catastrophic: seven lives lost in a preventable failure. The event remains a stark reminder of why *caution*, *careful evaluation*, and yes, *patience*, matter—especially when the stakes are high.

Another sobering example is the 1999 Mars Climate Orbiter. NASA's promising mission was derailed because teams failed to reconcile metric and imperial units—a mistake born, perhaps, from pressure and a lack of thorough review. The spacecraft and $327 million were lost. It's a powerful lesson in how a little *more patience*, a moment of *precision* and *clarity* could have changed the outcome entirely.

Patience, then, is not merely about enduring time—it's about cultivating a *mindful*, *resilient*, and *intentional* attitude throughout. Kant offers a timeless framework for seeing patience not as a passive wait but as a meaningful practice. When examined with care, our everyday lives reveal how challenging—and crucial—this virtue truly is.

In a fast-paced world, *embracing patience* can transform how we experience time, make decisions, and live peacefully. Life has a remarkable way of guiding us, even when we think we're simply taking a break. Perhaps we ought to listen more closely to those gentle nudges—and discover the *quiet beauty* of waiting with grace.

MANY FACES OF IMPATIENCE

In many traditional tribal cultures, performers or spiritual leaders often wear masks or paint their faces with detailed patterns, each representing a different *emotion*, *spirit*, or *role*. Take an Indian tradition, for example, where dancers performing classical dances like **Kathakali** use boldface makeup and costumes to embody various characters and emotions. Each face they wear tells a unique story: there is a **mask of anger**, a **mask of joy**, a **mask of sorrow**, and even a **mask of calm**. The colours and designs on their faces are not just for show—they communicate deep emotions and intentions to the audience. It is like they are stepping into a whole new world, using their faces to tell a story in the most powerful way possible.

I was thinking about this one day, and an image popped into my head—it hit me like a ton of bricks. Those painted faces? They were a lot like how I shift in different situations. When I'm racing to finish a script, I feel all *edges*, sharp and quick, my mind buzzing with impatience. In a meeting, I put on a *mask*, staying cool on the outside, but inside, I'm itching to get it over with. At home, I am restless, trying to find some calm, but it is like chasing shadows. Like the *Kathakali dancer*, I wear many faces—and so does impatience. It's not just one thing—it's a *symphony of shades*, each triggered by the people around me, my surroundings, and life's expectations. I have felt tension building when I'm trying to finish something by a deadline or twitching when everything feels like it's going too slow. You have probably worn those faces, too, right?

We all deal with impatience to some degree. We have all been there—waiting for something to happen and wishing it would hurry up. Whether it is waiting for a bus or waiting for your phone to load, we all struggle with it. We get frustrated when things move slowly, annoyed with delays, and sometimes even impatient with ourselves. The world is not moving fast enough, and we're constantly on edge, waiting for things to speed up.

So, what exactly is *impatience*? You get that feeling of frustration or restlessness when things are not going at the pace you expect or when reality does not match your mind. Imagine waiting for a late bus. You are tapping your foot, checking the time, and feeling increasingly irritated with every second. Your mind starts racing with all the other things you could be doing. That's *impatience* in action. It stops you from enjoying the moment and makes delays feel like a waste of time. Sometimes, it even shows up as irritability, like when you're stuck in a queue at the café, and the most minor inconvenience sets you off.

One type of *impatience* is **Emotional Impatience -The Fiery Red Mask**. This happens when you get all worked up because things aren't moving fast enough for your liking. For example, when a project you're working on is not progressing as quickly as you want, or when you're waiting for a colleague to reply to your email, and it feels like they have disappeared off the face of the earth and never been frustrated waiting for an email response? It has been an hour, and you start to feel anxious, even though you know you will get it eventually. That urgency we place on getting quick results builds unnecessary stress. Left unchecked, this *impatience* can turn into outright frustration, making you feel stuck and unable to move forward.

Then there is ***Cognitive Impatience - The Shadowed Black Mask***, where your mind cannot chill. You might be trying to focus on something—like reading a book—but your mind keeps wandering, thinking about all the other stuff you could be doing. You start thinking ahead, wondering when something will happen, making it hard to focus on what is correct before you. That feeling of constantly needing to be somewhere else? Yeah, that's *cognitive impatience*. It leads to restlessness, where your body feels agitated and your thoughts are racing. Your mind is always in overdrive, making it hard to relax and be in the moment.

Physical Impatience—The Jittery Yellow Mask is the most obvious one. You've probably caught yourself tapping your fingers, shifting in your seat, or checking your phone too often when waiting for something to happen. It's a physical response to the feeling that things should happen faster. I've fidgeted in meetings, checked the time a million times, or even impulsively bought something to distract myself from the discomfort of waiting. We all do it, but do not always notice that it reacts to *impatience*.

Social Impatience - The Bruised Blue Mask is another one that's become more common in our connected world. Do you know the feeling when someone does not reply to your message immediately? We expect everyone to be on the same page as us, answering instantly. This *impatience* can lead to frustration when social interactions move slower than we'd like. You might feel irritated while waiting for a friend to show up or anxious when someone takes too long in a conversation. It can even lead to worrying about why others have not replied yet and whether things are going as planned.

Technological Impatience - The Stark White Mask is something we have all probably felt. It's frustrating when your video starts buffering or when a webpage takes longer to load than you'd like. We're so used to technology being quick that even a tiny delay can drive us mad. It is funny how something as simple as waiting a few extra seconds feels like a massive problem. If you are not careful, this *impatience* can make you constantly dissatisfied with how fast technology works, affecting your mood and overall well-being.

Finally, there's **Productivity Impatience - Forces Fuelling Our Impatience.** This is when we rush through tasks, thinking that the faster we go, the more efficient we are. However, pushing ourselves to get things done faster often leads to burnout or poor results. Take writing an article, for example. If you rush through it to finish it quicker, you might miss important details or mess up the editing, making the whole thing subpar. Ironically, this can lead to procrastination because the pressure of getting things done quickly feels too overwhelming.

In all its forms, Impatience affects how we go about our daily lives and how we interact with others. Sometimes, it's natural to feel *impatient*, especially with everything moving so fast in the modern world. But learning to recognise and manage it can lead to more peaceful, productive moments. If we do not, *impatience* can spiral out of control, making us avoid things, criticise ourselves, and get caught up in negative self-talk.

So, the key is not to let *impatience* run the show but to learn to take a breath and manage it—sometimes, it is okay to wait. Managing impatience can bring a profound sense of relief, knowing you control your reactions and emotions and are not at the mercy of impatience.

IMPATIENCE – A DAILY IMPULSE

Every day, we encounter moments that test our patience—moments that, if left unchecked, can spiral into frustration and stress. It is almost as if impatience has become a reflex, an instinct we do not always control. Whether waiting for our morning coffee to brew, stuck in a never-ending line at the supermarket, or waiting for a slow email response at work, impatience has a sneaky way of showing up when we least expect it. It is as though life has become a race, and we are constantly worried about falling behind, even in the smallest of moments. I remember rushing to catch a train, and the person before me was taking their sweet time at the ticket counter. I felt my impatience rising, and it took a conscious effort to calm myself down and remind myself that sometimes, life takes time. You are not alone in this struggle.

Take this simple example: you're in a queue at the coffee shop, the line moving at a pace that seems absurdly slow. You start to shuffle your feet, tap your fingers on your phone, and glance at the clock—and before you know it, you are irritated, and that three-minute wait feels like an eternity. In those moments, impatience isn't just about the wait. It is a nudge in your mind, pushing you to get things done faster, to hurry up, and that feeling of restlessness can throw your whole mood off track. It is easy to forget that sometimes life takes time.

Then there is the moment when you send an email at work, ask a question, or make a request, and you do not get an immediate reply.

I Lack Patience

Your mind starts racing, your thoughts clouded with the assumption that something must be wrong, that people are ignoring you, or that you are being left behind. You refresh your inbox every few minutes as though the response will materialise just by sheer willpower. This, too, is impatience in its purest form—a demand for immediate responses in a world that does not always work on our timeline.

Social media makes this worse. We scroll through endless feeds, only to be bombarded with snippets of everyone else's *perfect lives*. It is like looking at a distant race and feeling like you are somehow lagging, even though you are unsure where the finish line is. The rush to keep up and get more likes, comments, and validation turns our daily online interactions into a competition against time, and patience feels like it is being slowly drained away with each post we scroll past.

Even at home, impatience finds its way into the equation. Have you ever asked your partner or kids to do something, and you find yourself tapping your foot, checking your watch, or sighing loudly when they do not do it fast enough? It's as if every little thing has to be done instantly, or else it's an inconvenience, an interruption to the day's schedule.

Yet, what if we paused and remembered that those moments of waiting—of 'slowing down'—are often the times we could take a breath and connect rather than rush through life like it is some race? These moments of waiting can be opportunities for self-connection and presence, making us feel more connected and present in our daily lives.

Impatience is a daily impulse that moves through us, whether caught in traffic or just trying to make dinner after a long day. Sometimes, it is a loud impulse, while other times, it whispers, but it is always there, tugging at us, asking us to hurry.

IMPATIENCE EPIDEMIC – *Struggle With Patience*

Nevertheless, what if, instead of racing against time, we learned to be more at ease with it? What if we recognised impatience for what it is—a signal, a trigger, that we need to slow down and tune in to the present moment? After all, *patience* isn't just the absence of impatience; it's the awareness that we're okay with things unfolding at their own pace.

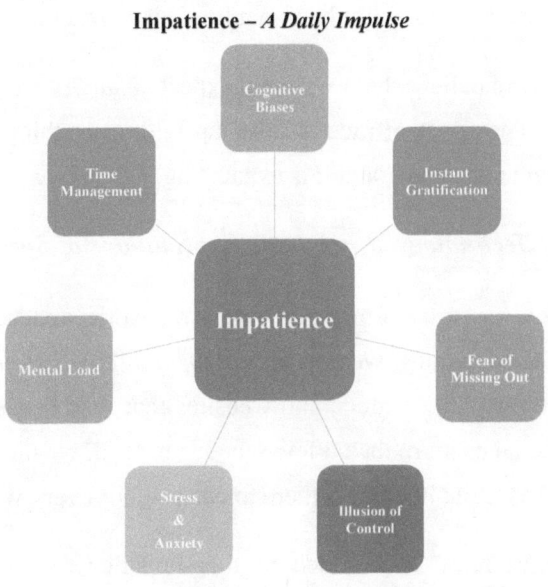

Impatience – *A Daily Impulse*

I encourage you to pay attention to your impatience as you go about your day. What triggers it? How does it make you feel? Furthermore, most importantly, how can you learn to be more patient with yourself and others? This self-awareness can be enlightening and empowering, putting you in the driver's seat of your well-being.

Living in the Fast Lane

I sometimes long for the old days when life felt *steady*, and we had time to breathe. However, today, we live in an age that *feeds impatience* at every turn, constantly pushing us to keep up with the rapid pace of life. The rise of *technological advancements, instant gratification* from online shopping and social media, and the pressure to stay productive have created a culture where speed is worshipped. We're stuck on a treadmill constantly speeding up, with the finish line out of reach.

We're made to believe that we should expect *immediate results* in every area of life. The constant race to keep up with everything leaves little room to breathe or reflect, and it is exhausting.

The Role of Technology: Unrealistic Expectations of Speed

Technology has transformed how we live, work, and communicate, and warped expectations. We now expect *instant replies* to emails, *same-day delivery* for online orders, and websites that load in a split second. When a page takes more than a few seconds to load, we mutter, *"This is ridiculous!"* as if the internet is there to cater to our every whim.

Smartphones have only added to this impatience, becoming little pockets of frustration that make us restless when they do not perform *lightning fast*. We have become so accustomed to instant responses that we cannot sit with things or allow space to *reflect* without feeling uneasy.

A study by *McKinsey* found that our *attention span* has decreased from 12 seconds in 2000 to just 8 seconds by 2013. We've become conditioned to consume information at *breakneck speed*, leaving little room for anything more profound or meaningful.

IMPATIENCE EPIDEMIC – *Struggle With Patience*

The Instant Gratification Culture: We Want It Now

The rise of e-commerce, same-day delivery, and *streaming services* has conditioned us to expect *instant gratification* in nearly every aspect of life. When we click *"Buy Now"* or *"Play"*, we expect immediate results. We feel irritated if they do not arrive—as time is against us.

Same-day delivery might seem like a godsend, but it teaches us that anything slower is unacceptable. This mentality extends beyond shopping. Today, we expect *instant replies* to texts and emails and even the swift resolution of our problems. When things don't happen at our pace, impatience takes over.

Social interactions are not immune to this either. We now expect *quick satisfaction* from conversations and get frustrated when someone does not respond immediately, whether a friend or colleague. This impatience is not just external—it also affects how we view ourselves, pushing us to meet our goals and timelines at *breakneck speed*. When we do not, we feel like we are falling behind.

Social Media and the Cult of Busyness: The Pressure to Keep Up

Social media has turned impatience into a *public performance*, with constant comparisons to others. We scroll through Instagram or Facebook and see curated glimpses of other people's success, productivity, and happiness, leaving us feeling inadequate when we think we're not moving fast enough.

The *"hustle culture"* glorifies the constant grind, making us believe that success only comes when we're always on the go. If we're not constantly ticking off tasks, we feel like we're failing. This creates a *rat race* where we feel guilty for taking breaks, even though we need them.

Success does not come from rushing. It comes from finding a balance between *productivity* and rest. In today's world, we've forgotten how to *stop* and breathe without feeling guilty. It's important to prioritise self-care and accept that taking a break is okay. This balance is not a luxury; it's a necessity for our mental and physical well-being.

The Consequences of Impatience: Beyond Frustration

Impatience has far-reaching consequences. When we rush through life at such a fast pace, we increase our *stress* and *anxiety*, making it impossible to relax genuinely. We end up in a constant state of *fight-or-flight*, and paradoxically, the faster we try to go, the less productive we become. We miss important details, like trying to bake a cake without preheating the oven—leading to a *half-baked result*.

Impatience does not just affect our productivity; it also seeps into our relationships. We find ourselves snapping at colleagues or friends for not responding quickly enough. Instead of building bridges, impatience often burns them. We become so focused on the next task that we forget to appreciate the *small victories*. Constantly rushing leads to *burnout*, and even our health suffers, contributing to *stress*, *anxiety*, and *hypertension* when impatience controls our lives.

THE CONTINUUM FRAMEWORK

You have probably come across the term *continuum* at some point, but if you have not, let me share how I stumbled upon it while researching ways to explain *impatience* and *patience*. I was wondering how to draw a line between the two, and that is when I came across the *Continuum Framework*. It is one of those ideas that's easier to grasp once you think about it in everyday terms. A continuum is a continuous range where things change gradually without clear-cut boundaries or abrupt shifts.

Picture a spectrum—like introversion and extroversion, where everyone sits somewhere in between rather than at one extreme. Or think of a rainbow—there is no sharp divide between the colours; they flow seamlessly from one to the next. In the same way, our experiences, emotions, and progress in life often exist on a continuum rather than as isolated points.

This concept is incredibly versatile and shows up everywhere. In *math*, for example, we have actual numbers with no gaps between values. In *philosophy*, time is often described as a continuum, with each moment flowing into the next without a break. Even our emotions can be seen this way: *happiness* and *sadness* exist on a scale rather than as opposites.

Why should we care about this? The *Continuum Framework* helps us understand that *growth*, *change*, or *development* does not happen in sharp, isolated steps. Instead, it is a gradual process—a continuous flow of shifts and adjustments over time. Things evolve step by step, not in one-off events. This perspective can reshape how we approach progress, patience, and success.

Let us look at a few examples where this idea fits:

- In *business*, innovation does not happen overnight. It is a continuous process—from brainstorming ideas to bringing them to life and scaling them over time.
- In *education*, learning is a gradual shift. Students move from beginner to expert, picking up skills and knowledge along the way, not in a straight line.

- In *healthcare*, think about the continuum of care. It is not just about fixing a problem once and then getting it done. It is about providing long-term support—treatment, rehabilitation, or maintaining good health.

Even in *mental health*, it is a continuum. From feeling balanced to dealing with stress or anxiety, mental health is not a yes-or-no thing. It is a spectrum, and we all move along it depending on what is happening in our lives.

To illustrate, let us consider the development of the *electric car*. This was not a one-time invention or an isolated breakthrough. It evolved gradually through decades of advancements in battery technology, government regulations, and consumer preferences—each step built on the last, from introducing hybrid models to fully electric vehicles like Tesla's. Today, we see the electric car as part of an innovation continuum—constantly improving, adapting, and scaling toward a sustainable future.

The beauty of the *Continuum Framework* is its flexibility. It allows us to measure progress, recognise where we are, and understand that change is a process, not an event. Whether personal, professional, or health-related, growth is a gradual transition, and moving through it step by step is perfectly okay. You do not have to rush to the end.

Think of this framework like a river. A river does not jump from its source to its mouth—it flows, sometimes fast, sometimes slow, carving its path through the landscape. Along the way, it gathers momentum, erodes obstacles, and nourishes its surroundings. In the same way, progress flows through our lives—gradually shaping us and moving us forward.

Impatience Epidemic – *Struggle With Patience*

So, next time you feel like you are not making progress fast enough, remember that change is often a slow, continuous journey, not a sprint. Embrace the process and trust the flow of your continuum.

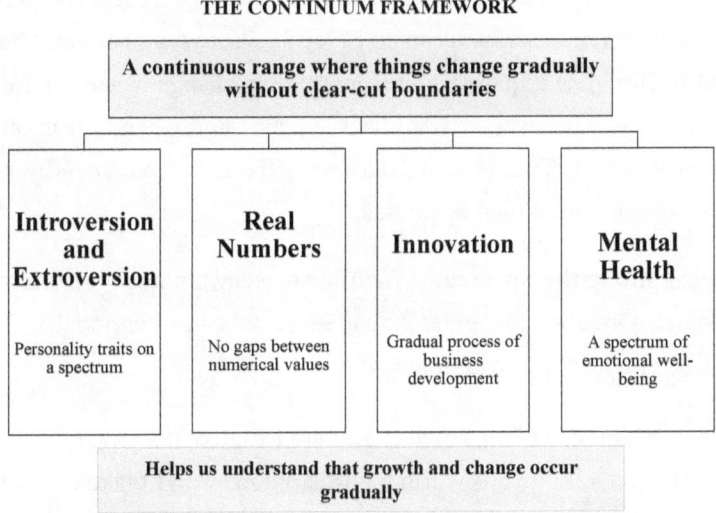

The Impatience-To-Patience Continuum Framework

Imagine *impatience* and *patience* as two ends of a continuum—more like a scale than fixed traits. On one end, you feel the pressure to rush, the frustration of waiting, and the need for instant results. Conversely, you can calmly wait, accept delays, and trust that things will unfold in time. Here is the crucial bit: this is not a fixed state.

Our position on the scale shifts constantly, depending on our awareness, mindset, and the techniques we practise. Think of this continuum as a line stretching across a vast landscape, with *impatience* on the left and *patience* on the right. Every situation places you somewhere along that line. Waiting for a cup of coffee might push you toward impatience, while sitting in traffic might nudge you closer to patience. It is like paddling a canoe—sometimes you fight the current, frustrated and struggling; other times, you float effortlessly, letting life carry you.

At its core, this is an empowering tool rooted in awareness and practice. With the right mindset, you can consciously shift your position. The goal is not to eliminate impatience; it signals when change is needed. Instead, it is about learning when to dial back urgency and when to lean into the present moment. This is about mastering the art of *patience* by taking charge of your emotional responses.

Shifting Along the Spectrum: We often need awareness to realise where we stand. Once we recognise impatience, we can intentionally change towards patience. For example:

- **Moment of Impatience**: You are irritated in a long queue. Ask yourself, "Is this worth the frustration? Can I make use of this time?"
- **Shift Towards Patience**: Instead of stewing in frustration, you take a deep breath, observe your surroundings, or practice mindfulness. By doing so, you nudge yourself closer to patience.

The more you practise this awareness and recalibration, the more naturally you shift your position. Over time, *patience* becomes less about willpower and more about habit—creating responses that place you further along the right side of the continuum.

Awareness vs. Impulse: *The Key to Shifting the Continuum*- Impatience feels automatic, driven by impulse. This is where awareness comes in. Once you recognise the impulse, you can choose how to respond. *Impatience* is not fixed—it is a reaction, and reactions can be managed.

IMPATIENCE EPIDEMIC – *Struggle With Patience*

Epictetus said, *"We cannot choose our external circumstances, but we can always choose how we respond to them."* Our ability to respond patiently lies within our control, even when impatience naturally rises. It's about pausing, reflecting, and acting from a place of calm.

Practice: *The Bridge Between Impatience and Patience*- Moving along the continuum requires awareness and *practice*. Every time you shift your mindset away from impatience, you build the muscle of *patience*. With consistent practice, the shift becomes easier. The more you lean into *patience*, the less impatience will affect you in those situations.

THE CONTINUUM FRAMEWORK

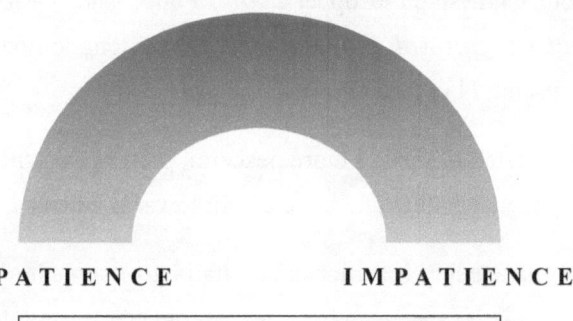

PATIENCE   IMPATIENCE

A continuous range where things change gradually without clear-cut boundaries

Over time, the shift feels less like a battle and more like a natural flow. As you face daily frustrations, the *patience* side of the continuum will feel more comfortable, and impatience will have less control. Your response will no longer be automatic but a conscious choice, helping you embrace challenges with grace and a more evident mindset. Remember, this is a gradual journey, and each step towards *patience* is a step towards a more balanced and fulfilling life. It's essential to be patient with yourself during this process, understanding that change takes time and every step forward is a victory.

The Power of Gradual Shifts

The beauty of the *Impatience-to-Patience Continuum* is that it does not demand perfection. It simply asks for *awareness* and *practice*. Over time, as you recognise where you are on the continuum and intentionally shift your position, you will notice that impatience becomes a less frequent visitor. You will naturally find yourself more patient without even trying.

The famous Chinese philosopher *Lao Tzu* once said, *"A journey of a thousand miles begins with a single step."* Like a long journey, patience is not built instantly but through small, consistent shifts.

We take each step towards a more peaceful, present existence by being aware of impatience and practising the shift towards patience.

So, rather than seeing impatience as a failing or something you need to eliminate, view it as a cue—a nudge that you can learn to move away from. This understanding can bring relief, as you realise that impatience is not a force to be reckoned with, but a signal to be heeded. With practice, you will find that you can embrace patience more often, creating a more peaceful, less hurried existence.

By shifting your focus from impatience to patience, you are changing how you respond now and reshaping how you experience time. Patience brings peace, reduces stress, and enhances relationships. It allows you to make better decisions and enjoy the journey rather than just the destination.

APPLYING THE CONTINUUM CONCEPT

The concept of the *Impatience-to-Patience Continuum* is not a widely recognised, formalised theory in psychology or philosophy and, thus, does not have a specific origin attributed to a single thinker or academic. However, it draws on several well-established psychological principles, frameworks, and insights from various fields, including behavioural psychology, mindfulness, and self-regulation.

That said, the idea of a continuum between two opposing states—such as impatience and patience—aligns with *continuum models* used in psychology and behavioural science, where traits or behaviours are understood not as binary but as existing on a spectrum. This model is often applied to emotions, cognitive states, and personality traits.

This framework is not rigid but dynamic, allowing for shifts along the scale depending on awareness and practice. Here is how it ties into existing theories and practices:

Psychological and Behavioural Foundations

Self-Regulation Theory: This theory suggests we can move along a spectrum from impulsive reactions (impatience) to more reflective responses (patience). For instance, Walter Mischel's *Marshmallow Test* highlights the shift between *instant* gratification (impatience) and *delayed* gratification (patience). It is a perfect example of developing patience as we move along the continuum.

Cognitive-behavioural therapy (CBT): CBT focuses on recognising and managing impulsive thoughts and behaviours. Using strategies to shift from knee-jerk impatience to more mindful patient responses, CBT works with this spectrum of emotional regulation.

Mindfulness and Meditation Practices

Mindfulness: Practitioners like Jon Kabat-Zinn encourage us to observe our thoughts and emotions *non-judgmentally*. This creates space to shift from impatience to patience, with the mindful pause allowing us to *reset* and cultivate a calmer response when impatience arises.

Buddhist Philosophy: Patience is a key virtue in Buddhist teachings, which focus on accepting the flow of life rather than forcing things to happen. Practices like meditation help to shift from *desire-driven* impatience to a state of peaceful acceptance.

Modern Applications in Business and Leadership

The continuum plays a significant role in leadership, especially in fast-paced environments. In *agile management*, leaders often must balance rapid decision-making (leaning towards impatience) with the strategic patience required for long-term planning. Stephen Covey's *The 7 Habits of Highly Effective People* promotes patience for significant goals while recognising the need for swift action in urgent situations, reflecting this dynamic balance.

In conclusion, the Impatience-to-Patience Continuum may not be a widely recognised theory, but it draws from a rich blend of philosophical and psychological frameworks. From Stoicism to modern mindfulness, its roots lie in *self-regulation, emotional awareness*, and *mindful practice*. By understanding where we stand on this continuum, we can better manage impatience and nurture patience—essential skills for thriving personally and professionally.

When applied to personal and professional growth, the transformative power of this continuum should inspire and motivate you to use these concepts in your life.

PRACTICAL EXERCISE: THE IMPATIENCE-TO-PATIENCE SHIFT

Objective: To help you identify moments of impatience in daily life, reflect on them, and consciously choose a more patient approach.

1. **Recognise the Trigger**:
- Start by noticing when impatience arises. This could be during activities like waiting in line, waiting for a reply to an email, or when you feel time is moving too slowly in any context. It could also be when you're stuck in traffic, waiting for a download, or when someone is taking too long to decide.
- When you feel impatient, pause for a moment. Take a deep breath and notice the thoughts or emotions that arise. Ask yourself: *What is triggering this impatience?*

2. **Assess the Situation**:
- Think about the situation from a different perspective. Is the wait necessary? What are the potential benefits of waiting? Are you in a rush, or are you more impatient about *how you feel* now?
- This step involves incorporating mindfulness into the equation—acknowledge the situation but do not react impulsively.

3. **Shift Your Mindset**:
Once you have recognised the impatience and assessed the situation, consciously move towards patience. Here are a few strategies:

- **Reframe the situation**: See it as an opportunity for growth, reflection, or relaxation. For example, while waiting in line, you might practice deep breathing instead of feeling frustrated or observing your environment.

- **Focus on the present**: Tune in to the *here and now*, even if it is something small like the sounds around you, the feeling of your body, or a sensation you would not typically notice when rushing.

- **Practice gratitude**: In moments of impatience, ask yourself what you are grateful for in the present moment—whether it is your health, your surroundings, or even the time to slow down.

4. **Reflect**:

- After the situation passes, reflect on how you responded. How did you feel before and after? Did you feel more at ease, or did impatience resurface again? Each reflection gives you insight into your emotional patterns and helps you grow in self-awareness.

- Over time, you can build this practice, and with each instance, you will notice a more remarkable ability to move towards patience instead of staying stuck in impatience.

ADVANCED EXERCISE: CREATING A PERSONAL PATIENCE MANTRA

Once you are familiar with your impatience triggers and how to shift towards patience, you can create a *personal patience mantra*—a simple phrase you repeat to yourself during moments of impatience. This could be something like:

IMPATIENCE EPIDEMIC – *Struggle With Patience*

- "In this moment, I choose to slow down."
- "Patience brings clarity."
- "Things unfold in their own time."

Repeating this mantra gently reminds you to be more patient in your response. It gradually moves you along the continuum of impatience to patience, where you can respond more calmly and thoughtfully.

2.
IMPATIENT ME – *Understanding My Triggers*

"The two most powerful warriors are patience and time." - Leo Tolstoy.

The word patience often feels like something from a fairy tale—a wise concept that seems distant in today's whirlwind world. We hear the phrase "patience is a virtue" often, yet few of us genuinely embody it. Most of us try to discipline ourselves to be patient, but there is always that nagging feeling that everything might fall apart if we do not hurry. Then there are those rare few who seem to glide through life as though the world is moving at their pace. For me, patience is not strictly tied to age.

While it is true that we tend to mellow with time, I believe patience is a skill that can be developed with practice, self-awareness, and the right mindset. The line between patience and impatience is often as thin as a hair—sometimes invisible, triggered by circumstances or our expectations.

Think about it: how often has impatience sneaked up on you? Whether it is the pressure of an urgent deadline, a never-coming phone call, or the

I Lack Patience

feeling that life is moving too slowly, we have all experienced frustration when the world does not match our pace. Often, the harder we try to control the situation, the more it slips out of our grasp.

Seneca, the ancient Stoic philosopher, captured this beautifully: *"We suffer more often in imagination than in reality"* (*On the Shortness of Life*, 49 AD). This insight speaks volumes. Much of our *impatience* and *anxiety is* rooted in our mental projections. We build worst-case scenarios in our minds, magnifying our fears before we even experience them. In reality, the outcome is rarely as dire as we imagined. By recognising this, we can start managing our thoughts and reducing unnecessary stress, allowing us to approach situations more calmly and clearly.

For me, impatience often arises from a few triggers: *expectations*, time pressure, and *lack of control*. One scenario where I feel this most acutely is when I am flying. It is not the long queues or the hours spent in the air that rattle me; it is the feeling of being entirely at the mercy of others. When I am sitting on a plane, I cannot help but feel restless. If I were flying the plane, I would feel in control, confident, and perhaps, ironically, more patient. However, as a passenger, I have no say in when we take off or how quickly we get there, and that uncertainty triggers a flood of anxiety. Another trigger for me is when I am stuck in traffic. The lack of control over the situation and the pressure of being late can be overwhelming. Does anyone else experience this?

This sense of *helplessness* is my trigger point. It often coincides with *time constraints* and life's unpredictability—when everything does not go as planned and my expectations crash against reality. That is when impatience takes root and frustration builds.

IMPATIENT ME – *Understanding My Triggers*

What I have come to realise is that *patience* is not just about waiting. It is about how we handle waiting. It is about the attitude we adopt during those moments of discomfort. Instead of seeing them as obstacles, we can reframe them as opportunities for *self-control* and *awareness*. Patience is not just about biding time but about *navigating* it calmly and purposefully.

In the end, *patience* is a practice—a deliberate choice to remain composed and resilient, no matter the circumstances. It is not about avoiding life's challenges but about learning to face them clearly and calmly, even when everything inside us screams to rush. The more we become aware of our *triggers*—a lack of control, time pressure, or unmet expectations—the better equipped we are to handle them. By understanding our impulses, we can consciously respond with *patience* rather than react with *impatience*.

So, what are your triggers? How do you manage your impatience in your daily life? We all face these challenges, but by cultivating *patience* and *self-awareness*, we can slowly transform how we navigate the world.

PATTERN OF IMPATIENCE

In 2011, Japan experienced a devastating earthquake and tsunami that caused widespread destruction. Despite the chaos and trauma, the Japanese people showed remarkable patience and resilience in rebuilding their communities. It was not just about enduring a disaster—a cultural response, a mindset of patience honed through centuries of hardship. This example underscores the deeply ingrained nature of patience and the extraordinary power of collective resilience in the face of calamity. It is a testament to the human spirit and a source of inspiration.

I Lack Patience

Impatience is a natural human emotion, often triggered by specific situations and environments. While it serves a purpose in navigating a fast-paced world, it can quickly become an obstacle to achieving goals and finding peace. The key is to recognise the patterns that trigger impatience—a particular environment, time of day, or state of mind—and learn to respond with mindfulness. This powerful tool empowers us to take control of our reactions and manage impatience effectively.

Let me share an experience that illustrates how impatience often creeps in. I was at the airport, which many of us dread because of its long queues, unpredictable delays, and crowded waiting areas. However, it was not the flight delay that got to me—it was the *lack of control*. I had no say in the departure time, no way to speed things up, and I could not predict how long the wait would be. As I sat there, shifting in my seat and checking the time, my mind raced with everything I could do—emails to send, work to finish, plans to make.

At that moment, I realised something crucial: impatience does not appear out of nowhere. It is triggered by a combination of *uncertainty*, *lack of control*, and *time pressure*—a pattern I had unconsciously rehearsed many times before.

The Common Triggers Of Impatience

This happens often, and I am sure it resonates with many others. Losing *patience* while waiting in *traffic* or snapping when someone is *late* usually brings *impatience* to the surface. Recognising these *triggers* is like turning on a light in a dark room—it helps us better understand and manage our *emotions*.

IMPATIENT ME – *Understanding My Triggers*

When stuck in heavy *traffic* on the way to an important *meeting*, frustration can quickly set in. The helpless feeling of being unable to control the situation is a common *trigger* for *impatience*. With so many other things you could be doing, your mind starts to race, and frustration builds. This **lack of control** only amplifies *impatience*, making it even harder to stay calm.

A remarkable example of managing this *lack of power* comes from the *Apollo 13 mission*. When an oxygen tank explosion crippled the spacecraft, the astronauts and mission control did not waste time panicking. Instead, they focused on what they *could* control—their response. This shows us that *patience* does not necessarily mean fixing the circumstances but managing our reactions with clarity and focus.

Do you feel your heart racing when running late for an appointment or staring at a deadline? **Time pressure** is another familiar culprit that triggers *impatience*. It is like trying to force a cake to rise faster by opening the oven door too soon—it does not help and often makes things worse. Does it sound like *time pressure*? Yes, it does.

Consider the 2004 *Indian Ocean tsunami*, where scientists had only 15 minutes to issue warnings. The stakes were life and death, and how they managed that immense pressure made all the difference. This example reminds us that it is not the clock itself but our ability to handle the anxiety of *time pressure* that determines our *patience* in high-stakes situations.

Have you ever waited for test results or tried to predict someone's reaction and felt frustrated? That is **uncertainty,** one of the sneakiest triggers of **impatience.** Philosopher *Søren Kierkegaard* called it "the dizziness of freedom," as we feel trapped between what could and is happening. Instead of being consumed by "what-ifs," learning to embrace *uncertainty* and stay grounded in the present moment can help us keep *impatience* at bay.

Have you noticed how your *impatience* skyrockets when you are exhausted? Sometimes, it is not the situation but how we feel inside. Mental, physical, or emotional exhaustion reduces our ability to regulate our responses. Even the slightest disruption can feel monumental when we are fatigued. That is what **mental and physical fatigue** does.

Research shows that when tired, we are more likely to seek instant gratification and less able to wait. Recognising when you are overextended and permitting yourself to rest can prevent *impatience* from spiralling into frustration.

I learnt to recognise my **patterns.** So, what about you? What triggers your *impatience*? Is it the *lack of control* in situations like traffic, the ticking clock of a deadline, the *uncertainty* of not knowing what is next, or simply feeling worn out? Everyone's *impatience triggers* are different, but they usually fall into one of these categories.

The key is recognising your patterns before they take hold. Reflect on those moments when *impatience* flared up—what was behind it? Once you identify these triggers, you can begin to shift your response.

Impatience does not have to be your default reaction. You can learn to pause, take a deep breath, and respond more comfortably with practice.

What if impatience *were not an automatic reflex?* What if you could reclaim that pause before reacting? Think of it like a space shuttle launch—it needs time to gather momentum before it can soar. Similarly, *patience* requires time to build. By pausing, breathing, and resetting your mindset, you can let *patience* guide you through life's chaotic moments.

IMPATIENT ME – *Understanding My Triggers*

As *Buddha* wisely said, "The greatest prayer is patience." Let *patience* be your compass, steering you towards calm and clarity, even when the world feels overwhelming.

SHAPING PATIENCE'S *PATH*

Ever find yourself in a situation where your patience seems to vanish? Moreover, it is not because you feel particularly irritable that day but because the environment is doing its best to test you. I am talking about those moments when the world around you deliberately pushes your buttons.

We tend to underestimate the power of *external factors*—our surroundings, the places we inhabit, the noises we hear. They play a massive role in shaping our emotional state, often more than we realise.

Our environment can be like a pressure cooker, a kitchen appliance that uses high pressure to cook food quickly. On the one hand, it can be a serene setting that soothes your soul, like a quiet lakeside or a peaceful park.

On the other hand, it can feel like the walls are closing in, like when you are in a bustling, crowded shopping mall, trying to keep your cool while your mind races. We often ignore how much these spaces influence us, but they do.

Familiar Environments That Trigger Impatience

Rush-Hour Traffic: The Slow-Motion Trap - Something about being stuck in traffic makes time feel like standing still. You are late for that crucial meeting, and the cars ahead barely move. You can see the clock ticking down, and the more you focus on it, the slower everything seems to go. You are caught between the *lack of control* (the traffic is not moving, and you cannot speed it up) and the *time pressure* (running out of time). It is like a perfect storm for frustration. Your patience? Drained.

Long Queues or Waiting Lines: The Waiting Game - Standing in line feels like time is taking a break while you are in the middle. It is not so much the wait—it is the *uncertainty* of how long it will last. Moreover, let us face it: the more you watch the clock, the more time seems to mock you. Whether at the grocery store, at the airport, or even at the post office, the feeling of a *lack of control* over the situation can push your patience to the brink.

However, here is the thing—waiting does not have to be a wasted moment. Reframe it. Use it as an opportunity to breathe, reflect, or practice mindfulness.

Noisy or Crowded Spaces: The Sensory Overload - Have you ever been on a crowded subway train at rush hour or tried to focus in a café full of chatty people? The noise, the movement, the constant bustle—like being in a pressure cooker of sensory overload.

This is the classic *lack of control* situation. You cannot control how loud the space is or how many people are there, but you can control how you react.

As Epictetus wisely said, *"We cannot choose our external circumstances, but we can always choose how we respond to them."* So next time you're surrounded by chaos, take a deep breath, centre yourself, and remember you can control your internal state, even if the world is swirling in a storm.

Impatient Me – *Understanding My Triggers*

High-Pressure Work Environments: The Deadline Race - Ah, the office—the place where deadlines are king, and the pressure is relentless. High-stakes work environments can feel like you're on a tightrope, balancing multiple tasks while the clock ticks away. The stress mounts, and before you know it, impatience starts creeping in, urging you to rush through things.

However, here's the catch: rushing through tasks creates more stress and mistakes. Patience in these environments is like a muscle—it needs practice. When you feel the urge to panic or rush, take a step back, breathe, and focus on explicit, thoughtful action.

Patience In Adversity

So, how do you handle those impatience-inducing environments? Imagine being stuck in traffic or waiting in an endless queue—it is easy to let frustration take over. However, here's the thing: while you cannot control the environment, you can control your reaction. Let us explore simple strategies to help you navigate these situations calmly and clearly.

Reframe the Situation*:* Picture this—you are in a long queue, and time is standing still. Instead of letting annoyance creep in, consider the moment a chance to pause. Use that time to reflect, breathe, or even brainstorm ideas for something you have been putting off. Waiting in line could be your unexpected productivity boost. Think of it like a pause button in the game of life—a moment to reset before diving back in.

Breathe and Reset*:* Never underestimate the power of a few deep breaths. When impatience strikes, your breath can act like a life raft, pulling you out of the storm of frustration. Imagine your breath as a reset button—a quick way to clear the mental clutter and regain emotional control. Next time you feel impatience building, take a moment to inhale deeply, hold it for a few seconds, and exhale slowly. It is like giving your mind a mini-holiday.

Set Realistic Expectations: Not everything is within your control—traffic will crawl, queues will stretch, and deadlines will loom. Instead of battling against these inevitabilities, focus on what you can control: your reaction. Think of it like being a sailor in rough seas—you cannot stop the waves, but adjust your sails. Accepting that some things are out of your hands can help you navigate the situation without losing your cool.

Shift Your Focus: When impatience hits, sometimes the best strategy is distraction. Picture a photographer zooming out to capture the bigger picture. Whether diving into a book, listening to your favourite playlist, or visualising your long-term goals, shifting your focus can help break the cycle of frustration.

By looking beyond the immediate problem, you can find a sense of calm amidst the chaos.

Managing impatience does not have to be complicated. It is about recognising when frustration is taking over and using simple tools to bring yourself back to balance. These strategies—reframing the situation, breathing, setting realistic expectations, and shifting focus—are like a toolkit for staying calm in challenging environments. Remember, patience is a skill you can build, one small step at a time.

Final Thoughts: Environment is Everything. Picture your patience like a plant—it needs the right conditions to thrive. Too much noise, stress, or chaos, and it wilts. However, it can bloom even in less-than-ideal spaces with the right mindset. Though your surroundings might test your patience, they do not have to dictate your mood.

It is not the environment that makes you impatient; how you respond to it matters. This reiteration of the power of choice in responding to the environment can make you feel more empowered and in control of your emotional state.

So, the next time you find yourself stuck in traffic, waiting in a long queue, or trapped in a noisy space, take a moment to pause. You have the power to navigate through it with a calm mind.

Your environment does not have to control your emotional state—patience can be the anchor that keeps you steady, no matter what is going on around you. It's a superpower that you possess, waiting to be unleashed.

Psychological Impact - *The Hidden Mental Toll*

Impatience is not just an emotional reaction—it can have serious psychological and physical effects. Understanding this is like turning on a light in a dark room, revealing the sneaky gremlin that quietly tightens the threads of *anxiety*, *stress*, and even *muscle tension*, often without us realising it. While impatience may seem harmless, it is more like a *pressure cooker*, steadily building psychological heat that can explode.

The Anxiety and Stress Connection

When impatience takes hold, it doesn't just affect our emotions; it spills over into our bodies. Imagine you're waiting for something important, like a job interview result. The longer you wait, the more your mind races, and before you know it, your *heart rate* quickens, your *breathing* becomes shallow, and your muscles tighten. This happens because impatience triggers your body's *fight-or-flight response*, even if there's no real danger. It's your brain signalling that something's wrong—*but is it?*

Anticipating delays or uncertainty—even for small things like waiting for an elevator—raises cortisol levels, increasing tension. Your *physical state* mirrors your *mental state*: frazzled, tense, and on edge.

Mental Projections: Imagining the Worst-Case Scenario

A big reason impatience feels so overwhelming is how we mentally project ourselves into the future. When we're impatient, our minds go into overdrive, imagining the worst. Rather than accepting the present moment, we begin to spin out potential disasters.

For example, when waiting to hear back from a job application, your mind races with thoughts like, *What if I don't get it? What if they don't like me?* These mental *doom scenarios* amplify impatience and fuel anxiety. You're not just reacting to the now but crafting a fictional future based on fear.

This *mental spiral* can become a self-fulfilling prophecy, where your anxiety amplifies impatience, and your patience evaporates. It's like being stuck in a car with the engine revving but not moving anywhere.

Assumptions: Building Bridges to Stress

Assumptions are another powerful fuel for impatience. We often assume things are going wrong before they even do. Take an *office deadline*, for example. You might think the worst as the clock ticks down: *What if the boss hates my work? What if I missed something crucial?*

IMPATIENT ME – *Understanding My Triggers*

These assumptions snowball into stress, turning a manageable situation into a *pressure cooker* of worry. The more you think about the *worst-case scenarios*, the less you focus on solving the problem, and your patience continues to shrink.

The same happens with *high-stakes meetings* or *business fallouts*. You imagine the client walking out or failing to deliver. These mental *what-ifs* make you rush, cut corners, and lose focus, all because you have already convinced yourself that failure is inevitable.

Overthinking: The Silent Engine of Impatience

Impatience and overthinking often go hand in hand. It is like your mind cannot stop rehearsing the worst possible outcomes. Overthinking drags you into a mental storm, magnifying your fear and uncertainty. Overthinking feeds the fire, whether it is job stability, financial worries, or relationships.

What if I lose my job? What if my business collapses? These *what-ifs* build on one another, preventing you from acting calmly or thinking clearly. The more you overthink, the more mental chaos you create, deepening the *stress*.

In these situations, impatience is not about wanting things to speed up but trying to outrun your thoughts. The more you overthink, the harder it becomes to tackle the challenges before you and the deeper the mental strain.

The Vicious Cycle: Impatience and Mental Health

This constant loop of *assumptions*, *overthinking*, and *mental projections* creates a dangerous cycle. The more impatient you become, the more stress builds up, and over time, it can lead to burnout, *anxiety*, or even *depression*. Your emotional bandwidth, or the capacity to deal with emotional stress, shrinks as you juggle these spiralling thoughts, and soon, you are caught in a trap of frustration and exhaustion.

In high-pressure environments, whether a *deadline*, a *critical meeting*, or *personal challenges*, impatience can create a *psychological barricade*, preventing you from being productive or at peace.

Managing Impatience: Shifting from Overthinking to Action

The key to managing impatience is to break the cycle of overthinking. Rather than imagining the worst-case scenarios, shift your focus to the present moment and the actions you can take right now.

For instance, if you are waiting for a response, use the time to work on other tasks or hobbies. Focus on *small wins*, not the giant leaps.

Recognising that *assumptions* and *overthinking* fuel impatience helps you regain control. Remember, patience is not about forcing things to happen on your timeline—it's about trusting the process and adapting to uncertainty.

Final Thought: Patience as a Tool for Mental Well-being

Impatience isn't just about wanting things faster—it's a *psychological time bomb* triggered by assumptions, mental projections, and overthinking. It creates a mental loop that fuels stress, anxiety, and tension.

The next time impatience creeps in, take a moment to pause, breathe, and reset. In these moments, patience is not just a virtue; it's a tool for *mental clarity* and *emotional resilience*. Managing impatience can help you break the cycle and protect your mental health.

IMPATIENT ME – *Understanding My Triggers*

REFRAMING IMPATIENCE - *SHIFTING PERSPECTIVE*

Impatience is often seen as a *villain* that pulls us away from our goals and adds unnecessary stress to our lives. But what if impatience were more like an *untapped resource*? What if, instead of pushing against it, we could harness it for growth? By shifting our perspective, we can transform impatience into a powerful tool for *self-control*, *self-awareness*, and more transparent decision-making, empowering us to take charge of our emotions and actions.

The Power of Reframing

Reframing is a simple yet profound technique that allows us to change how we perceive a situation. Instead of seeing impatience as something negative or debilitating, we can view it as an opportunity to *pause*, reflect, and improve our emotional intelligence.

Take the example of being stuck in a traffic jam. It's easy to get frustrated and let impatience take over, but here's where reframing can work wonders. Rather than allowing the situation to push us into a spiral of frustration, we can *reframe* it by turning it into an opportunity to:

- ☐ Please take a few deep breaths and calm yourself down
- ☐ Listen to music or a podcast
- ☐ Reflect on our day, making plans for what comes next
- ☐ Enjoy the rare moment of *quiet time* to ourselves

By reframing such situations, what could have been a *stressful, energy-draining moment* becomes a *chance for mindfulness*. This leads to a sense of calm and clarity rather than frustration, providing much-needed relief from the usual stress.

I Lack Patience

Patience as a Tool for Self-Control and Self-Awareness

Many of us think of patience as a passive quality—it is just about waiting calmly, right? However, patience is a *powerful tool* for building self-control and enhancing self-awareness. When faced with challenges, impatience often pushes us to act impulsively, but patience allows us to pause, reassess, and respond more thoughtfully.

Imagine you are working on a project and encountering an unexpected obstacle. Rather than letting impatience push you into *rash decisions*, you could take a step back, breathe, and assess the situation. This gives you the space to:

- ☐ Identify the *root cause* of the problem
- ☐ Develop a *strategy* to overcome the obstacle
- ☐ Stay focused on your broader *goals*

Using patience in this way helps you build greater resilience, stay on track, and ultimately achieve *tremendous success*. It does this by controlling the impulse to rush and act without thinking, giving you a sense of accomplishment and control over your actions.

Patience as a Mindset for Composed Decision-Making

Patience is not just a reaction; it can also be a mindset that allows us to remain composed, even when the pressure is high. In moments of stress or conflict, it is easy to get caught up in the heat of the moment, but patience helps us step back, consider our options, and respond with clarity.

For example, picture yourself in a meeting where someone presents an idea you strongly disagree with. The *instinct* might be to react immediately, to argue your point right there and then. However, with patience, you can choose to:

- Take a deep breath, listen to the other person's perspective, and allow the conversation to unfold
- Respond in a calm, thoughtful manner rather than a defensive one
- Develop a deeper understanding of the situation before making any decision

This ability to remain composed and think helps avoid unnecessary conflict and leads to better, more thoughtful decision-making in both professional and personal contexts.

Conclusion: Patience as a Positive Force

Impatience is a *natural human emotion*; in many ways, it's an unavoidable part of life. However, by reframing impatience as an opportunity for growth, using patience as a tool for self-control and self-awareness, and cultivating it as a mindset for composed decision-making, we can transform impatience into something *positive*—a force that drives us forward rather than holding us back. This shift in perspective empowers us to take control of our emotional responses and use impatience as a catalyst for personal growth.

So, the next time impatience starts to creep in, try to shift your perspective. Ask yourself: How can I use this moment for growth? How can I turn this frustration into a *moment of clarity*? With patience, we don't just wait—we grow, reflect, and move forward with purpose.

I Lack Patience

What are your thoughts on reframing impatience? How do you use patience to improve self-control and decision-making? Share your experiences!

Patience Is A Practise, Not A Trait

Patience isn't something we're born with—it's a skill that can be *cultivated* and refined over time. It's easy to think of patience as a *fixed trait* you either have or don't. However, the truth is, like any other skill, it can be developed through conscious effort and regular practice. By embracing patience daily, we can experience *personal growth*, greater *clarity*, and more profound *long-term satisfaction*.

This empowerment lets us control our emotional responses rather than be at impatience's mercy.

Patience is a Skill to Cultivate

Rather than seeing impatience as something that "just happens," we can shift our perspective and view patience as a tool we can *train*. For instance, when you're faced with a situation that typically triggers impatience—like waiting in a long queue, dealing with a slow email response, or waiting for a delayed flight—practice slowing down your mind and pausing before reacting.

You can also practice patience in everyday situations like traffic jams, long meetings, or dealing with a difficult person. The more we consciously choose to remain calm, the more we build our capacity for patience.

Like building muscle at the gym, *patience* strengthens the more we practice it. Over time, we react less impulsively and approach challenges more excellently.

The Daily Practice of Patience

Making a daily effort to practise patience doesn't mean forcing ourselves to endure unpleasant situations in silence. Instead, it's about intentionally cultivating a mindset that values *restraint* and *awareness* of overreaction. Small moments—being patient with a colleague, ourselves, or during moments of stress—become opportunities to train this skill. With time, this practice leads to:

- *Personal growth*: We learn to respond to situations thoughtfully rather than impulsively.
- *Greater clarity*: Patience lets us step back and assess the situation before making decisions.
- *Long-term satisfaction*: By practising patience, we become less focused on instant gratification, learning to appreciate the journey rather than just the destination

How Patience Improves Relationships and Wellbeing

The benefits of cultivating patience extend far beyond personal growth. Developing patience also helps to build stronger, more resilient relationships. Patience fosters empathy, understanding, and mutual respect in our friendships, -family dynamics, or work relationships. Instead of reacting defensively or getting frustrated by others, we learn to *listen*, *wait*, and respond thoughtfully and supportively. For instance, patience can help you navigate disagreements with colleagues in a work setting.

In contrast, in a family setting, it can help you understand and support a family member going through a tough time.

Patience is not just a virtue; it's a powerful tool for reducing stress and improving mental well-being. When we're patient with ourselves, we're less likely to be overwhelmed by feelings of inadequacy or frustration. We also become more resilient in the face of challenges, knowing that we can deal with setbacks without spiralling into anxiety. This emphasis on the role of patience in reducing stress and improving mental well-being can make the audience feel more at peace and less overwhelmed.

Conclusion: Patience as a Lifelong Practice

Patience isn't a passive trait—it's a lifelong practice. By consistently cultivating patience, we enhance our ability to stay calm under pressure, make better decisions, and nurture healthier relationships. As we develop this skill, we create a *foundation of peace* and *mental well-being* that leads to a more fulfilling life. However, it's important to note that cultivating patience is not always easy. There will be times when impatience seems to be the easier path. But we can continue our personal growth and patience journey by acknowledging these challenges and developing strategies to overcome them.

Case Study: Amazon's 1-Click Ordering

Turning Impatience Into Innovation

In the early 2000s, Amazon's CEO, Jeff Bezos, wanted to revolutionise online shopping by introducing the *1-Click Ordering* feature, allowing customers to make purchases with just one click. However, the team faced significant challenges: tight deadlines, complex technology, and increasing pressure, leading to *impatience* and frustration.

Bezos reframed their impatience by shifting the focus away from the delays and toward the *customer experience*. He encouraged the team to think about how the feature would simplify the shopping process, making it easier and faster for customers to buy. This change in perspective motivated the team to overcome obstacles and focus on creating a seamless, *user-friendly* experience.

The result was a game-changing feature that improved the customer experience, drove higher *conversion rates*, and increased sales. *1-Click Ordering* became a hallmark of Amazon's platform and set a new standard for the e-commerce industry.

This case shows how reframing impatience and focusing on a greater goal—like improving the *customer journey*—can transform frustration into innovation. Bezos turned the team's impatience into a powerful motivator, demonstrating that we can overcome challenges and create groundbreaking solutions by focusing on long-term objectives.

3.
WHY WE RUSH – *Unpacking The Roots*

"The best leaders are those who can balance speed and patience." - John Maxwell.

During the *Crimean War* of 1854, British cavalry units, led by Lord Cardigan, charged directly into heavily fortified *Russian artillery* positions. What followed was a catastrophic loss for the British forces, and the charge has since become one of the most infamous military blunders in history. At the heart of this tragedy was a combination of *impatience* and poor communication.

The British commanders, eager for a swift and decisive victory, failed to fully assess the situation. Instead of taking the time to evaluate the complexities of the battlefield, they rushed into action, driven by the pressing need to achieve a quick win. This hasty decision, made without considering the risks or alternative strategies, resulted in disastrous consequences.

Though we may never know the exact reasons behind this fateful charge, one thing is clear: *impatience* played a significant role in the failure. *Patience*, after all, is often cultivated through *discipline, experience,* and

I Lack Patience

wisdom—qualities built over time. *External pressures* likely contributed to the commanders' decision, but at its core, the failure to exercise patience ultimately resulted in irreversible consequences.

As we reflect on this event, we might question its motivations. Still, one thing remains certain: *patience* is not something we have—we develop through careful consideration, reflection, and learning from *experience*. *On the other hand, Impatience* is an impulse that can cloud our judgment, especially in moments of high pressure.

In many ways, this historical example mirrors our everyday experiences with *impatience*. Whether waiting for a cup of coffee to brew, sitting in traffic, or waiting for an important email to arrive, we all encounter moments when our *patience* is put to the test.

So why does *impatience* feel so overwhelming at times? Is it just a result of living in a *fast-paced world*, or are there deeper reasons behind our frustration? In this chapter, we'll explore the roots of *impatience* and the factors that trigger it. Much like untangling a knot, understanding *impatience* can bring relief. Tracing its origins requires us to investigate, but once we do, we can begin to unravel its complexities.

PATIENCE PUZZLES – TRIGGERS AND INFLUENCES

Have you ever had one of those days when you're feeling calm and collected, but the next day, the tiniest delay makes you want to explode? *Impatience* can be a real puzzle—it doesn't just appear out of nowhere. Many factors contribute to it, often hidden beneath the surface.

Why We Rush – *Unpacking The Roots*

Take my own experience, for example. After wrapping up *Navigating the Grey*, I promised myself I'd take a break. I was exhausted, ready to step back and relax. Yet, not long after, I found myself back at my laptop, chasing the next idea. Why? I think part of it is how I was brought up. My dad always said, "If you are not doing something, you're wasting time." That mentality stuck with me, and now, even when I need rest, I feel the urge to jump straight back into work.

It is also the world we live in. Society is obsessed with speed. Think about those ads offering *"next-day delivery"* or the short, snappy social media videos designed to capture our attention instantly. It's no surprise that we have come to expect everything to happen straight away. And then there are the environments we find ourselves in—a deadline-heavy office or a home where the kettle is taking forever and the kids are running riot. These things amplify our *impatience*, sometimes before we even realise it.

What about you? Did your family encourage a fast-paced lifestyle? Does your day feel like a never-ending rush to get things done? These early influences, coupled with the pressures of our surroundings, are where *impatience* often takes root. But it's not just about those irritating moments—it's about understanding why we lose our *patience*.

The Past Haunts Us. *Impatience* often has its roots in our upbringing. If you grew up in an environment where everything was rushed and there was always a sense of urgency to complete tasks, you likely developed a low tolerance for delays. Maybe your parents were always on the go, or the pace of life around you never slowed. Over time, this urgency becomes ingrained, and waiting feels uncomfortable and almost unbearable.

I Lack Patience

Personality Traits. It's also worth noting that some people are naturally less *patient* than others. If you thrive on action, constantly moving from one task to the next, you might find it frustrating when things slow down. *Patience* might feel like a distant concept you struggle to make room for. It is not necessarily about your circumstances; sometimes, it's simply how your *personality* is wired.

Chaotic Environments. Have you ever felt like everything around you is in chaos? These environments can fuel impatience, whether in a stressful workplace with constant pressure or a home where things are always in disarray. When your surroundings are chaotic, your *patience* tends to wear thin. With so much going on, delays or disruptions feel like additional burdens, making *impatience* even more challenging to manage.

Understanding the origins of impatience is crucial to managing it effectively. It is not just about those moments when you're waiting for a coffee to brew or stuck in traffic—it is about recognising the patterns in your past, your *personality*, and your environment that influence how you react. Once we identify these triggers, we can begin to address them, making it easier to navigate impatience and manage life's delays.

The Perfect Trap

Do you ever think everything has to be spot-on, or it's simply not worth doing? I've been there. While writing *Navigating the Grey*, I would spend hours tweaking a single sentence, chasing some elusive version of *perfection* in my head.

Why We Rush – *Unpacking The Roots*

If it were not right, I would get twitchy—*impatience* creeping in because the reality didn't match my sky-high standards. It's like setting yourself up for a fall.

Perfectionism and *Unrealistic Expectations*

One of the biggest culprits behind *impatience* is *perfectionism*. We've all done it—expecting a project to be flawless immediately or wanting others to meet our high expectations without a hitch. But life, as we know, is messy. When we hold ourselves—or others—to these *impossible* standards, impatience sneaks in when things do not go according to plan.

I recall spending over an hour fussing over a single paragraph—every word had to be *perfect*. My wife walked in, saw me glaring at the screen, and laughed. "It's fine as it is—give it a break," she said. She was right, but I couldn't let it go. That's when *impatience* took over—chasing a finish line that didn't exist. The truth is that *perfection* is an illusion. Part of learning *patience* is accepting that things won't always go perfectly, and that's fine.

FOMO and the *Instant Fix*

Then there is the modern beast that's always lurking: **FOMO**—*fear of missing out*—and the constant craving for *instant gratification*. After finishing my book, I felt it big time. Everyone on social media seemed to be posting about their latest wins—new projects, holidays, you name it. And there I was, feeling like I had to keep up.

The worry that you're falling behind? That is a fundamental driver of *impatience*.

I LACK PATIENCE

Now, picture this: you're scrolling through Instagram and seeing a mate has just finished their novel. Suddenly, you are itching to start your next project. Or you are waiting for a reply to a text, and five minutes feels like an eternity because you want that *instant buzz*. It's all part of *FOMO* and the addiction to *quick fixes*. Whether it's the buzz of a like on a post or a speedy takeaway delivery, it's easy to get hooked on the idea of now—and that's jet fuel for *impatience*.

The Need for Instant Gratification

Alongside *FOMO*, the culture of *instant gratification* has made our *patience* thinner. From social media to shopping apps, we're constantly conditioned to expect everything instantly. A slight delay can feel unbearable, whether it's waiting for a buffering video or an email reply.

However, here's the kicker: delayed gratification—staying committed and working towards something—often leads to a much more satisfying outcome. Recognising this is key to overcoming *impatience*.

We live in an age where everything is just a click away—whether it's food delivery, an online shopping spree, or an instant-loading video. Waiting has become a challenge.

The problem is that *FOMO* fuels this *impatience*. We feel like we're missing out if things don't happen immediately, but rushing through life to avoid this only makes us miss the present moment.

So, the next time you're feeling *impatient*, remember that sometimes it's about slowing down to truly appreciate the process, rather than rushing through it in search of an *instant fix*.

Why We Rush – *Unpacking The Roots*

Patience isn't just about waiting—it's about being mindful of how we spend our time and learning to let go of those *unrealistic expectations* that leave us restless.

The Fallout – How Impatience Hits Home

Let's get real—*impatience* doesn't just stay in your head; it spills over into your life. One evening, I'm feeling restless because my wife's taking her time sorting dinner plans, and I snap—silly, really, over something so small. That's *impatience* ruining the vibe, and it is not just her who feels it. I'm kicking myself, feeling like I've let us both down. It's a quiet thief—it steals your *calm*, strains your relationships, and even erodes your self-perception.

You've probably felt it too—getting irritated with a mate for dawdling, only to feel daft when you find out they had a good reason. Alternatively, rushing through something—like those endless edits—only to end up frazzled with a shoddy result. That's *impatience* costing you *peace*, personal growth, and meaningful conversations with the people who matter most. Tackling it is about more than just avoiding a bad mood— it's about becoming a steadier, happier version of yourself.

Charting Impatience's Sparks

I've lost count of how many times I've written in a frenzy, only to go back and find glaring mistakes that shout *haste*. One instance that always comes to mind is when I rushed to finish a report for work because I was behind on other deadlines. I submitted it, feeling satisfied with how fast

I Lack Patience

I'd worked, only to have it come back full of errors. It taught me that rushing doesn't just waste time—it also costs me *peace of mind*. This kind of *impatience* has its roots in deep-seated issues. A famous example of *haste* leading to disaster dates back to the 1960s, with the discovery of *polywater*.

Scientists rushed to publish their findings on a new form of water, and in their haste, they overlooked the possibility of contamination. Instead of revolutionising science, it set back the field, wasting resources and damaging the trust in scientific progress (Franks, 1981). It's a perfect example of how *impatience* can create more problems than it solves.

Like these scientists, we often race through our lives, missing the small yet essential moments that could lead to *personal growth*. Whether it's sending off a half-finished draft or impatiently waiting for your food at a busy restaurant, the rush often clouds our *judgment*. But here's the kicker: realising what ignites *impatience* in us is the first step to understanding it—and ultimately, taming it.

For me, it's the constant hum of relentless pace, work deadlines, and life's unyielding churn. However, identifying the root causes of my *impatience* is changing how I approach everything from work to relationships. So, let's uncover your triggers together and start stepping toward *patience*—one spark at a time.

Tracking Your Triggers. Have you ever found yourself tapping your foot, looking at the clock, or muttering when something doesn't go as planned? Maybe a *traffic jam*, a colleague's slow reply, or a delayed flight? I've had my fair share of these moments. But I've learned that instead of reacting immediately, it's better to notice what triggers *impatience* and write it down.

WHY WE RUSH – *Unpacking The Roots*

Several months ago, I found myself caught in a notorious *traffic* jam. As the minutes stretched into what felt like an eternity, I could feel my irritation mounting. Ordinarily, I would have succumbed to frustration, blaming the world for my misfortune. But this time, I took out my phone and noted: "What triggered my *impatience* today?" The answer? Time was "lost". This feeling of wasted time is one of my primary triggers.

Daniel Kahneman, a psychologist and Nobel laureate, writes that our brains are wired to seek immediate rewards, making us *impatient* with anything that slows us down. It's a basic human instinct—our minds crave the quickest possible path to gratification. But by becoming aware of my triggers, I can start to gain more control. The relief of identifying these triggers is immense, and I want to share with you a sense of empowerment.

Start by doing the same. Keep a small notebook or a note on your phone. Write down what sets off your *impatience*—a slow queue at the coffee shop or someone taking forever to answer your message. Notice how you react—do you sigh? Tap your fingers? These little details can help you pinpoint patterns. Once you identify your triggers, you can begin to address them. It's like finding the source of the storm so you can weather it better.

Mindfulness: A Moment to Breathe. *We* often hear about mindfulness, but don't always embrace it. When stuck in *traffic* or waiting in line, we may feel the urge to lash out or get frustrated. But what if, instead of reacting immediately, we took a pause?

A few weeks ago, I found myself in a situation where an app I was using froze during an important meeting. The old me would have gotten frustrated and kept tapping away at my phone, trying to get it to work. But this time, I paused. I took a deep breath, focused on the present moment, and let go of the urge to fix the problem immediately. And, believe it or not, it helped.

According to the *Dalai Lama*, *"Patience is the ability to remain undisturbed."* In today's world, where everything moves at a million miles per hour—between honking cars, constant notifications, and endless deadlines—it's easy to get swept up in the rush. But *mindfulness* offers a way to slow down and reclaim some calm.

A study by psychologist *John Kabat-Zinn* demonstrates that mindfulness—simply paying attention to one's thoughts and breath—can help reduce stress and enhance decision-making. The sense of calm that mindfulness can bring is reassuring, and it's a tool that I encourage you to explore in your journey towards patience.

Subsequently, when *impatience* starts creeping in—whether in a stalled meeting or waiting for your order to arrive—try taking 10 seconds to breathe deeply and notice your thoughts. It's not about making the situation go faster; it's about gaining the ability to decide how you'll respond.

Self-Compassion: A Kind Response. We all struggle with *impatience*, but often, the real damage occurs when we berate ourselves for feeling impatient. Have you ever thought, "Why am I so *impatient*?" or "I should be better than this." These thoughts only make things worse. Being hard on yourself doesn't make you more *patient*—it just piles on the stress.

A recent example from my life occurred when I became frustrated with a *chai* vendor. He took longer than usual to prepare my tea, and I snapped at him in my rush. I had a headache, and I wanted tea *immediately*—maybe it's my way of excusing that tea would relieve my headache. Each person has their approach to finding solutions; for me, tea works. I walked away feeling terrible. But instead of dwelling on it, I took a moment to practice *self-compassion*. I told myself, "It was a rough moment, but I'll handle things better next time." Rather than spiralling into frustration, I forgave myself and moved on.

Psychologists such as Kristin Neff emphasize the importance of self-compassion in enhancing emotional well-being. When we respond to ourselves with kindness instead of criticism, we reduce feelings of anxiety and increase our ability to handle stress.

So, next time *impatience* strikes, try this: instead of chastising yourself, say, "It's alright, I'm learning." You'll be surprised at how much lighter it makes you feel. The importance of self-compassion cannot be overstated, and it's a practice that can make you feel understood and accepted, even in moments of impatience.

Unearthing the Roots. *Impatience* doesn't come out of nowhere—it's usually rooted in something more profound. That "stay busy" voice comes from Dad, who's always been on the go. It's a *cultural* thing, too, especially in fast-paced places. The constant push to move quickly is almost ingrained in the air.

Perfectionism has also played its part. I would spend hours on my scripts, obsessing over every word. It was about getting everything right, but I learned this often resulted in more stress and less satisfaction.

I'm not the only one who struggles with *perfectionism*. Look at *Elizabeth Holmes*, the founder of *Theranos*. She rushed to build a revolutionary blood-testing company, faked results, and caused massive harm—all because she couldn't accept delays or imperfections (Carreyrou, 2018).

I Lack Patience

So, I've started making tiny shifts. For example, I aim for a solid first draft instead of creating a perfect one. It takes the pressure off and lets me move forward. I've also started reducing my screen time to reduce *FOMO*—that feeling of missing out when I see others living a more exciting life. By making these small changes, I'm learning to embrace *patience* in a world that constantly pushes for speed.

The Reward: Why Patience is Worth It. So, why bother with all this? Why invest time in understanding your *impatience* and practising *patience*? Once you start identifying your triggers, it's like finding the anchor in a storm. Understanding why I felt *rushed*—due to external influence and the world's fast pace—has made me feel a lot more at peace. It's not about eliminating *impatience* but lightening the load. I'm editing more calmly, letting minor delays slide by, and even smiling when things don't go as planned.

Polywater damaged trust in science; *Theranos* destroyed lives, and my *rush* cost me peace. But recognising my triggers—like those moments when I feel time is slipping away—has helped me find steadiness. Building patience is worth it in a world that moves too fast—not for perfection, but for a calmer, saner life. What could cultivating *patience* open up for you?

Onward We Go. Next, we'll work on reshaping those *impatient* reactions. For now, start by tracing your triggers. Write them down, breathe through the frustration, and be kind to yourself. I'm no expert; I still race ahead sometimes, but recognising why— improvised hyped pace, my *perfectionism*—has started to shift the tide.

You're human, living in a "now" world. Each trigger you identify is one step closer to becoming the *patient*, grounded person you want to be. Ready to start?

WHY WE RUSH – *Unpacking The Roots*

ROOTING OUT IMPATIENCE

Addressing *impatience* is not an insurmountable challenge; it can be effectively managed through straightforward strategies. Having grappled with this myself—most notably after completing *Navigating the Grey*, when I found myself unable to rest despite my intentions—I've identified several practical approaches that yield results. These methods, refined through personal experience, offer a clear path to understanding and overcoming *impatience*.

Recognising Triggers – Understanding What Ignites Impatience

To manage *impatience*, one must first identify its triggers. This became apparent when, after submitting my manuscript, I hovered over my inbox, restless for a reply—a habit that left me perpetually on edge. The solution lies in observation: monitor the situations that provoke frustration, be it a delayed response, a slow queue, or a faltering internet connection. You can discern patterns over a few days by recording these moments—perhaps in a notebook or phone. This awareness empowers you to anticipate and address *impatience* before it takes hold, much like preparing for a storm that is known to be coming.

- **Practical Step:** When *impatience* stirs, note the trigger—such as "delayed train"—and your reaction. Reviewing this will help you identify your key catalysts.

Embracing Self-Compassion – Offering Kindness Amidst Impatience

A cornerstone of managing *impatience* is *self-compassion*. I once found myself pacing anxiously over an editor's tardy response, silently berating myself for my lack of calm. My wife's gentle remark—"You've no *patience*, have you?"—prompted a shift. I began to think, "This restlessness is natural; I'm still learning." This act of kindness towards oneself reduces the strain that fuels *impatience*. Rather than viewing such feelings as a flaw, recognise them as part of the human experience. *Self-compassion* paves a quiet road to *patience*, easing the internal pressure that often accompanies delays.

> ☐ **Actionable Advice:** In moments of *impatience*, affirm, *"It's understandable to feel this way; I am progressing."* This fosters calm and resilience.

Setting Realistic Expectations – Releasing the Burden of Perfection

Impatience often stems from unattainable standards. While drafting *Navigating the Grey*, I would labour over a single sentence, chasing perfection, only to grow frustrated when it eluded me swiftly. I learned to set "good enough" goals—solid drafts rather than flawless ones—and the relief was palpable. This approach applies beyond writing: accept that plans may falter, and outcomes need not be impeccable. As *Albert Einstein* observed, *"Strive not to be a success, but rather to be of value."* By embracing realistic expectations, you free yourself from the urgency of perfection, allowing *patience* to flourish in its place.

> ☐ **Simple Practice:** Aim for "effective" rather than "perfect" for your next task—observe how this diminishes *impatience*.

Practising Delayed Gratification – Building Patience Through Waiting

The modern craving for *instant rewards* amplifies *impatience*. I have felt this keenly—scrolling social media, seeing others' successes, and itching to leap into my next project, driven by a fear of missing out. Yet, I've found value in resisting this urge. Instead of checking my phone at the first hint of boredom, I might wait and take a short walk. My wife once suggested, "How about a breather outside?"—a wise alternative to the scroll. *Viktor Frankl* noted, *"Between stimulus and response, there is a space. In that space, it is our power to choose our response."* Practising delayed *gratification* strengthens this space, enhancing *patience* over time.

- **Effective Method:** When tempted by an immediate action—like checking a message—pause for five minutes. This slight delay builds endurance.

Employing Mindfulness and *Breathing – Restoring Calm to Counter Impatience*

Impatience often escalates with *stress*, a pairing I've encountered frequently. Once, a faltering Wi-Fi connection during research nearly unravelled me—until I paused, took three deep breaths (four *seconds* in, four out), and reset my focus. On another occasion, a late delivery prompted me to step outside briefly, breathing steadily by the window. *Jon Kabat-Zinn* aptly stated, *"You can't stop the waves, but you can learn to surf."* These *mindfulness* and *breathing* exercises provide a simple, immediate tool to halt *impatience*'s momentum, fostering a composed mindset conducive to *patience*.

- **Practical Technique:** When *impatience* rises, take three slow breaths—four seconds in, four out. This restores equilibrium swiftly.

Integrating these practical strategies into your life allows you to manage your *impatience* more effectively. It's about being kind to yourself, setting

I Lack Patience

realistic expectations, and taking small steps to improve. Over time, these efforts will help you handle delays and challenges more patiently, making your day-to-day life feel calmer and more manageable.

With consistent practice and self-reflection, you'll find that your ability to manage impatience will grow stronger, enabling you to approach life's challenges with a more composed and thoughtful mindset.

Case Study:
The Development of the Tesla Model's

The Tesla Model S, a groundbreaking electric car, faced significant delays during its development, including supply chain issues, battery technology setbacks, and manufacturing difficulties. Despite the pressure to deliver on time, Tesla's leadership reframed these delays as opportunities to improve the car's design and technology. Elon Musk, who admitted that impatience had led to moments of doubt, recognised that rushing would compromise the car's quality and Tesla's long-term reputation.

Instead of succumbing to impatience, Tesla took the extra time to refine the car's performance, integrate cutting-edge battery technology, and perfect the design. This strategic approach ultimately paid off, as the Model S, released in 2012, exceeded design, performance, and battery efficiency expectations.

Key Takeaways:

1. Reframing delays as opportunities alleviates impatience and fosters a strategic approach.
2. Taking time to improve processes leads to higher-quality outcomes.
3. Strategic patience, combined with innovation, can drive long-term success.

When we take the time to improve processes, we achieve higher-quality outcomes and a sense of pride and accomplishment. It's a testament to our dedication and patience.

4.
COST OF IMPATIENCE – *How Frustration Affects My Life*

"Patience is not about being slow; it's about being strategic." – Unknown.

Consider the life of *Michelangelo*, who, when painting the *Sistine Chapel* ceiling, endured countless hours of painstaking work. He often spent days lying on his back, meticulously painting each section of the canvas. The masterpiece did not emerge from hurried effort but from sustained *patience* and a clear vision. Like a sculptor carving away at marble, *patience* allowed Michelangelo to unveil beauty, depth, and detail that couldn't be rushed. The same goes for any outstanding achievement—whether in art, work, or life—*patience* is the quiet force that makes it possible.

Impatience is a subtle thief—it creeps in quietly, but its impact can be profound. I have felt its weight, and I imagine you have, too. It often starts as a minor frustration or a brief irritation, but *impatience* can disrupt much more than we realise when unchecked. This chapter isn't just about pointing out the damage it causes; it's about understanding how it undermines our lives, from the little annoyances to the more immense, more significant consequences.

At first glance, *impatience* might seem like a fleeting feeling, a burst of frustration that passes quickly. However, over time, the long-term effects of impatience and frustration can have a ripple effect, influencing our decisions, relationships, and overall well-being. We might dismiss it now, but when *impatience* goes unchecked, it can lead to severe costs—both big and small.

As *Albert Einstein* wisely said, *"A calm and modest life brings more happiness than the pursuit of success combined with constant restlessness."* His words remind us that success isn't about rushing to the finish line. It's about taking the time to be thoughtful, deliberate, and *patient*. When we slow down and appreciate the process, the results are often more meaningful, lasting, and fulfilling.

The Personal Price – When Impatience Robs Me of Peace

Let me start with a confession: a repetitive thought has been running through my mind as I write this. After finishing *Navigating the Grey*, I was knackered—and promised myself a proper break. But I hunched over my laptop before long, itching to dive into the next project. My wife caught me at it and, with a gentle nudge, said, "You've no *patience*, have you?" That hit me like a ton of bricks. That restless itch? It is *impatience* robbing me of my peace. I'd snap at her over the tiniest things—like her taking a minute too long to sort dinner plans—then feel awful straight after. It is not just the moment; it lingers, gnawing at my mind and stealing my sense of calm. I've also experienced impatience in my professional life,

Cost of Impatience – *How Frustration Affects My Life*

rushing through tasks and making mistakes that could have been avoided with a more patient approach.

The philosopher Seneca once said, "Nothing is so bitter that a calm mind cannot find comfort in it." But *impatience* strips away that calm and leaves nothing but frustration. I have rushed through edits, only to spot typos later—wasting hours fixing something that could have been avoided if I had just taken my time. It's a vicious cycle: *impatience* leads to stress, stress leads to mistakes, and mistakes pile on even more frustration. Have you ever huffed at a slow cooker or messed up a job because you could not wait? Impatience is costing you not just time but your inner peace.

Impatience and frustration are not just fleeting feelings—they can snowball into stress, anxiety, and even burnout. The constant pressure of rushing through tasks and demanding immediate results keeps you on edge, constantly chasing the next thing to do. Over time, this relentless *impatience* can leave you emotionally drained and disconnected from the present. The need to "get things done" clouds my judgment, causing me to overlook crucial steps that could enhance the quality of my work. It's like trying to speed through life, only to realise you've missed out on what matters. However, when we take a step back, embrace patience, and slow down, we can make more thoughtful decisions, improve the quality of our work, and reclaim the peace that *impatience* has quietly taken away.

The Ripple Effect – *How Impatience Strains Connections*

Impatience does not just affect me—it spills over into the lives of those around me. One evening, after a long day, I became impatient because my wife took longer than usual to decide on a takeaway. I snapped over

I Lack Patience

something trivial, and immediately, the mood shifted. She didn't deserve that, and I felt awful afterwards. Impatience can often undermine the relationships we care about most. It can lead to arguments over insignificant matters, cause tension during decision-making processes, and even result in hurtful words being spoken. But when we embrace patience, we can make decisions with confidence and reassurance, knowing that we have taken the time to consider all aspects and make the best choice.

Impatience can damage personal relationships, negatively impact productivity, and create tension in the workplace. Rushing tasks or reacting harshly to others only increases stress and makes everything feel like a chore. Over time, this continuous pressure and frustration can lead to feelings of anxiety and burnout, both at work and in life. It is a cycle that can be difficult to break, but it is crucial to recognise how deeply it affects us.

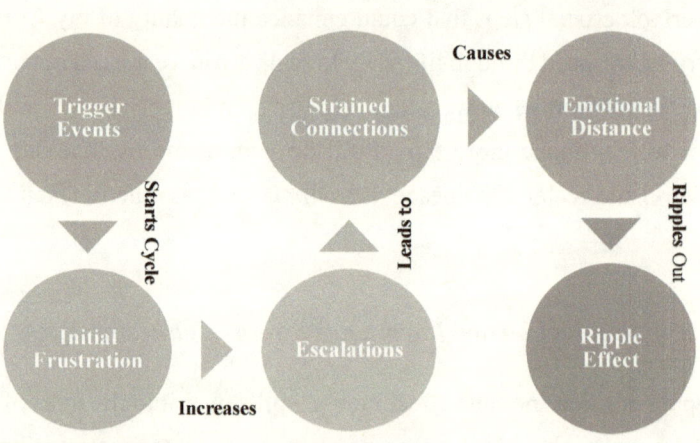

The Ripple Effect – How Impatience Strains Connections

COST OF IMPATIENCE – *How Frustration Affects My Life*

Looking at history, *impatience* has had devastating consequences. During the *Second World War*, the Allies rushed to capture a bridge over the Rhine—Rhein crossing to push troops across quickly. The bridge was hastily patched up, and although it held for ten days, it eventually collapsed, resulting in lost lives and a delay in their advance. Fast-forward to modern times: In 2018, the *Florida International University* bridge, constructed in a rush using an untested method, tragically collapsed, killing six. *Impatience*—whether in wartime or today's world—has a heavy price, affecting everything from personal relationships to the infrastructure we rely on.

THE HIDDEN TOLL – STUNTING GROWTH AND WELL-BEING

The cost of *impatience* extends beyond frustration—it can hinder our personal growth and overall well-being. I have certainly felt it firsthand. After wrapping up *Navigating the Grey*, I was able to push through and complete the next task. I skipped breaks, believing speed was key, but all that led to burnout and a draft of mistakes. *Carol Dweck*, who developed the concept of *a growth mindset*, rightly said, *"The view you adopt for yourself profoundly affects the way you lead your life."* When *impatience* takes over, we are trapped in a *fixed mindset*, constantly trying to avoid delays instead of learning from them.

Impatience harms work and our health. The constant pressure to do everything quickly can cause stress, disrupt our sleep, and leave us feeling drained. It is like trying to sprint a marathon—it is unsustainable and can lead to emotional and physical exhaustion.

History also provides stark reminders of the dangers of rushing into decisions. The *Titanic*, once hailed as the epitome of modern engineering, was pushed to set sail before it was fully ready for sea. The rush to get the ship in the water meant there were not enough lifeboats, and the result was one of the most tragic maritime disasters, claiming over 1,500 lives. In recent times, the Samsung Galaxy Note 7 was rushed to market, resulting in battery issues that led to explosions. The *company's impatience to meet a release deadline cost it* billions and severely damaged its brand. Whether in our personal lives or the corporate world, *impatience* can undermine our peace, stall our progress, and jeopardise our health and success.

THE PATIENCE PYRAMID

To understand how *patience* is developed, think of it as a pyramid. Each pyramid step represents a growth layer, building upon the one below it. Like any other skill, *patience* does not happen overnight—it's cultivated gradually, piece by piece.

At the base of the pyramid lies *self-awareness*. This is where it all begins. Before being patient, we first need to recognise when we are impatient. It's about noticing those feelings of frustration or irritation when things don't go according to plan. Once you become aware of your impatience, you can start making choices about how to respond.

Building on self-awareness comes emotional regulation. At this level, we learn to manage our reactions, acknowledging that impatience is natural but choosing not to let it control us. It is about stepping back and recognising that our feelings do not have to dictate our actions. This could be as simple as taking a deep breath or stepping away from a situation to gather our thoughts.

Above emotional regulation, you have mindfulness. This is the practice of being fully present in the moment without rushing or wishing for things to be different. Mindfulness enables us to break the cycle of impatience before it begins, allowing us to stay grounded even in frustrating situations. It is a skill that requires regular practice, but over time, it will enable us to respond to life's challenges with a calm and clear mind.

At the top of the pyramid lies compassion—for ourselves and others. When we reach this level, we understand that impatience is not something to fight or suppress; it is a natural part of our experience. Instead, we embrace it as part of our human experience. We acknowledge that we all make mistakes, face delays, and experience frustration, but these moments are growth opportunities, not reasons for self-criticism.

THE PATIENCE PYRAMID

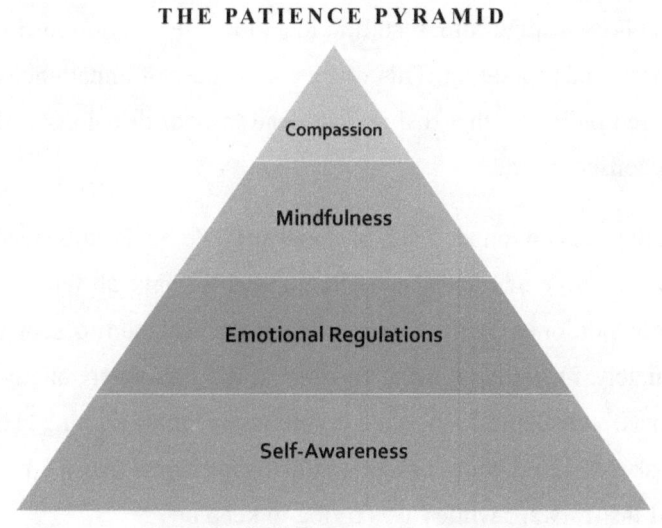

So, where are you on the *patience pyramid*? Are you just starting to become aware of your impatience, or are you working on developing your emotional regulation and mindfulness? Reflecting on this helps you see where to focus your efforts to climb the pyramid and cultivate more *patience*.

Remember, climbing the pyramid is not about perfection—it is about progress. Each small step brings you closer to a more patient, calm, and resilient version of yourself. And, just like any skill, you will improve with regular practice. So, start where you are and take the first step up the pyramid today.

The Modern Dilemma of Impatience

In 2016, Samsung's rush to outpace Apple led to the disastrous release of the Galaxy Note 7. Due to poor quality control and rushed testing, several phones caught fire, resulting in a global recall, billions in losses, and a damaged reputation. This was a classic case of impatience costing dearly, reminding us that rushing can lead to poor decisions with long-lasting consequences.

Impatience is no longer just a personal struggle but is embedded in our society. The pace of life has accelerated, and we have all felt its impact. We are conditioned to want everything from fast food to social media immediately. I have felt it myself—after working tirelessly on my books, I promised a break but soon found myself at my laptop, itching to start the next task. My mind could not slow down, and it was like the world had pressed fast-forward while I was trying to keep up.

Cost of Impatience – *How Frustration Affects My Life*

Then there is my son, who was raised in the digital age. Everything is instant for him—a new phone or a credit card. When he turned 18, he asked for one, completely bypassing any patience for the process. To him, everything should be available now, and this impatience is part of a more significant issue: the digital world has conditioned a whole generation to expect everything with the tap of a finger.

Social media has played a considerable role in this. We post something, hoping for likes and validation, and impatience takes over when we don't receive it quickly enough. I have scrolled through Instagram, comparing my progress with others and feeling restless when I do not see quick results. Social media feeds into this constant need for *immediate gratification*— we are all in a race to prove we are doing something worthwhile, and the waiting game feels obsolete.

Streaming services like Netflix have only made this worse. Gone are the days of waiting for weekly episodes of a show; now, we binge-watch entire seasons in one go. It is convenient, but it has shortened my attention span, making it harder to focus on slower-paced activities like reading. The *instant gratification* culture has invaded our leisure time, making it hard to sit still and appreciate the moment.

Instant messaging is another culprit. I have found myself constantly refreshing my inbox, expecting quick replies. My son does the same—he texts and expects an instant response, even when I'm busy. This pressure to always be "on" is draining, creating a sense of urgency that's hard to escape. *I recall a time when I was so engrossed in a writing project that my son kept texting me. The Constant interruptions were frustrating, and I realised how our* tech has evolved, but we have not learned how to deal with the constant rush it creates.

Then there is the *gig economy*—the culture of always hustling, where individuals take on short-term, freelance work rather than traditional full-time jobs. I have dabbled in it myself, trying to juggle multiple writing projects. The pressure to always be working, producing, and earning leaves little room for rest and relaxation. It is the impatience to achieve success fast, but it comes at the cost of personal time, well-being, and proper recovery.

Urban life adds stress. Long commutes, crowded trains, traffic jams—it's all part of fast-paced city life. I've been stuck in traffic, frustrated by how slow everything is; yet, the more I rush, the more I miss the little moments that truly matter. Impatience breeds frustration, which can be exhausting.

Comparison and envy are everywhere. Social media highlights everyone's best moments, making it hard not to feel like we are falling behind. I have felt the pressure to keep up with other writers, seeing them hit milestones and wondering why I'm not moving as quickly. This constant race leads to impatience, burnout, and frustration, eroding our ability to appreciate where we are in our journey.

The *Grenfell Tower* tragedy in 2017 is a chilling example of what happens when impatience takes precedence over quality and safety. In a rush to complete the building, cheaper, flammable materials were used, leading to a disaster that claimed 72 lives. The impatience to finish quickly, at the expense of safety and proper planning, resulted in a tragedy that could have been avoided.

Now, we live in a world where *impatience* is the norm. The pressure to always be on the go and consistently produce is exhausting. It costs

Cost of Impatience – *How Frustration Affects My Life*

us more than we realise—our *health*, relationships, and *peace of mind*. Trying to keep up, we are losing sight of what matters.

The real question is: Are we ready to slow down? Are we prepared to step back, appreciate the process, and cultivate patience as a valuable asset for ourselves and society? If we continue to race ahead, we will miss the most essential aspects of life. But if we choose patience, we enrich our personal lives and contribute to a more balanced and harmonious society.

Measuring the Cost – Are You Impatient? A Quick Check

So, how do you know if *impatience is* running your show? I have put together a little test—nothing fancy, just a way to take stock. Grab a pen and tally your answers:

Self-Assessment: The *Impatience* Gauge

1. When waiting, do you often tap your foot or check the clock? (Yes/No)
2. Have you snapped at someone over a slight delay in the past week? (Yes/No)
3. Do you rush tasks and then spot mistakes later? (Yes/No)
4. Does a slow internet signal or queue make you feel restless? (Yes/No)
5. Do you feel behind if you're not always doing something? (Yes/No)

Scoring:

- 0-1 Yes: You're pretty steady—*patience* is your mate.
- 2-3 Yes: *Impatience* pops in now and then—worth a look.
- 4-5 Yes: It's got a grip—time to tackle it head-on.

I Lack Patience

I scored a four the first time—tapping, snapping, rushing, the lot. Eye-opener, that. Try it yourself—be honest, no one's judging.

Shifting the Tide - Exercises to Build *Patience*

Knowing the cost is one thing; taking action is another.
Here are a few simple, practical exercises I have learned that can help you develop patience. Think of them as tools for fixing a leaky pipe—minor tweaks make a big difference.

1. The Five-Minute Wait

- *What:* Next time you are itching for a quick win—like checking a text—wait five minutes.
- *Why:* It builds *delayed gratification*. I held off checking my phone mid-draft, which calmed the buzz in my head.
- *How:* Set a timer if it helps—it may seem daft, but it works.

2. Breathe Through It

- *What:* When *impatience* flares—say, Wi-Fi's lagging—take three slow breaths (four in, four out).
- *Why:* Resets stress, as Jon Kabat-Zinn says: "You can't stop the waves, but you can learn to surf." I did this when the post was late—it kept me sane.
- *How:* Stand still and focus on the air. It takes ten seconds.

3. Reframe the Hold-Up

- *What:* See a delay as a chance—stuck in a queue? Plan your day instead of stewing.

- *Why:* Shifts perspective. I started jotting ideas when traffic stalled—turned drag into a win.
- *How:* Ask, "What can I do with this time?"—flips frustration to purpose.

4. The *Patience* Log

- *What:* For a day, note one moment you stayed calm—e.g., "Didn't huff at the slow cooker."
- *Why:* Tracks progress builds a *growth mindset*. Dweck's right—small wins grow you.
- *How:* Scribble it down—build a habit of spotting *patience*.

Impatience costs us more than we realise—robbing us of peace, straining relationships, and hindering growth. But every step towards patience reclaims calm and connection. For me, it's been about pacing less and finding more balance, and it has been worth every bit of effort. The journey towards patience is not just about reclaiming peace but also about personal growth and resilience. Try it for yourself—the rewards are worth the wait.

THE CONSEQUENCES OF MODERN IMPATIENCE

The cumulative effect of these modern dilemmas can have far-reaching consequences. Some of the most common effects include:

- *Increased stress and anxiety*: The constant rush for instant results contributes to heightened levels of stress.

- *Decreased attention span*: Relying on instant gratification leads to difficulty focusing on longer tasks or projects.
- *Poor mental and physical health*: The pressures of living in an impatient world can result in burnout and exhaustion.
- *Strained relationships*: *Impatience* with others can lead to misunderstandings, arguments, and a breakdown in communication.
- *Decreased productivity and performance*: Rushing through tasks or avoiding proper planning often results in lower-quality outcomes.
- *Increased burnout and exhaustion*: The relentless pace of modern life, combined with *impatience*, can cause physical and emotional fatigue.

Case Study: Miyawaki method of reforestation - A Long-Term Commitment to Growth

One of the best examples of patience in action is the practice of tree planting. It's a slow, long-term investment that requires years, sometimes decades, before the full benefits are realised. Take the case of the famous Miyawaki reforestation method, pioneered by Japanese botanist Dr. Akira Miyawaki. The technique involves planting native species densely and in layers, thereby mimicking the structure of natural forests. However, the real test of patience lies in waiting for these trees to mature and become part of a thriving ecosystem.

In 2006, Tokyo initiated a massive urban forest planting project using this method. At the time, critics wondered if this would even work, given the time it takes for trees to grow. Fast-forward to today, these urban forests have created green spaces that not only cool the city but also improve air quality and biodiversity. The key here was patience—allowing the trees the time they needed to grow and flourish without rushing the process.

The Miyawaki method shows how patience is a powerful tool for long-term success. It was not about instant results but rather a steady commitment to planting and nurturing something that would take time to mature. Over the years, this patience has paid off, providing numerous environmental benefits for generations to come. This story of patience and perseverance is a testament to the enduring rewards of patience.

Similarly, when I reflect on my journey with writing—whether creating complex fictional worlds or delving into the intricate layers of a nonfiction piece—I often find myself rushing, wanting instant results. But when I remember the tree plantation story, I'm reminded that good things take time, and the process is just as valuable as the result.

5.
SOCIAL FACTORS – *A Patience Trap*

"We suffer more often in imagination than in reality." Seneca.

Let us rewind to a time when the world moved much slower. The *Industrial Revolution*, which began in the mid-18th century and lasted into the early 19th century, marked a massive shift in human history. The world was transitioning from an agrarian economy, where people lived and worked in accordance with the rhythms of nature, to one dominated by factories, machines, and mass production. While bringing immense progress, this shift also meant that workers had to adapt to a much faster pace—dictated by the seasons and the factory clock.

For the first time, people were expected to work quickly, without pause, and the pressures of this newly industrialised world gave birth to a sense of *impatience* that had not been seen before. In those early days, impatience began to take root as workers rushed to meet deadlines, often at the expense of their well-being and mental peace.

This pressure to act quickly and efficiently in the face of the industry was not entirely new to humanity. Patience has long been regarded as

I LACK PATIENCE

a virtue, especially in ancient teachings. *Buddhism*, for example, has been encouraging *mindfulness* and *patience* for over 2,500 years. In its teachings, patience was not just a passive waiting game but an active practice of awareness and calm acceptance of the present moment.

It's a reminder that the art of patience, rooted in reflection and understanding, has coexisted with us for millennia. As we navigate the modern world, it's crucial to engage in self-reflection and understand the role of patience in our lives.

Jumping to the present day, the *Digital Age*—the new era of *impatience*—has only amplified this sense of impatience. We live in a world where everything is available instantly—whether it's food, entertainment, or information. The rise of smartphones and *social media* has conditioned us to expect immediate responses via text, email, or social media posts. I've often found myself impatiently refreshing my inbox or waiting for feedback on a project, only to feel more stressed when I don't get the instant results I'm looking for.

It is not just me, either. My son, raised in the *digital age*, constantly seeks the next gadget or upgrade as soon as it hits the market. The idea of waiting for something, of working for it over time, is a concept that feels alien to him. Everything should be immediate to him, as it often is in the world he grew up in.

The truth is, it's not just individual *willpower* at play here. Society itself shapes how we experience impatience. From *family expectations* to societal pressures to succeed to the relentless *urban pace* and the pull of *instant connectivity*, we're surrounded by forces that push us to be faster, quicker, and more productive. This culture of *immediacy* can be draining and frustrating, yet it's woven into the very fabric of modern life. As much as we may try to resist, external pressures influence how we think, how we work, and even how we relate to one another.

So, what is the takeaway here? It's not just about *slowing down* for peace, but also about understanding how our social surroundings—familial, professional, or digital—impact our *patience and tolerance*. From the pressure to keep up with societal expectations to the constant connectivity of the digital age, we live in a world that often moves too fast for us to appreciate the moments that genuinely matter.

The real question is about slowing down and *reclaiming patience* in a world that constantly pulls us in the opposite direction. As you read through this, I hope you'll start to notice how these social forces impact your life and think about how you might begin to slow down amidst the rush.

Rushing to Results – *Workplace Success*

Work can be a *pressure cooker*, no doubt. *Deadlines*, *quotas*, and the constant rush to achieve set targets test our *patience* in ways that often lead to *mistakes* and *burnout*. I've been there myself—pushing through late nights to meet tight deadlines, only to end up with *scripts* full of errors, my body and mind completely *exhausted*. It is a quick-fix mentality, prioritising speed over *accuracy*, and the long-term consequences often follow.

Take my mate, for example. He is a *chef*, and a while ago, he rushed a dish to meet the high expectations of a *Michelin guide* reviewer. The result? He lost the opportunity for a *Michelin star*. Now, he approaches his work more patiently, taking the time to perfect every dish. And you

I LACK PATIENCE

know what? His *reputation* has skyrocketed since. It is a lesson in the value of *patience*—taking the time to get it right brings greater rewards in the long run.

Contrast this with my son's approach to work. Raised in the *digital age*, he's all about *instant gratification*—his freelance *gig apps* are about making money quickly. "I want cash now, no waiting," he says. He's not alone in this rush to earn immediately; it's a mindset prevalent in the *gig economy* and modern *work culture*.

Then there is the larger picture—the *Boeing 737 MAX disaster* of 2019. In their rush to compete with *Airbus*, Boeing skipped crucial safety checks, and we all know how that ended—two crashes, 346 lives lost, and billions of dollars in damage. *Impatience* in the workplace can have devastating consequences when pushed to the extreme.

However, the flip side is also true—*patience* can lead to success. A *coder* I know spent months perfecting an app, carefully building it with every detail in mind. When it finally launched, it was a hit. *Patience* paid off.

Yuval Noah Harari—a historian and author of books such as *Sapiens*—has a point when he says, "Modern economies run on impatience"—*speed* is the god we serve.

We've all felt the pressure, whether churning out work for an *editor* who wanted a draft yesterday or struggling to meet *Amazon's* insane warehouse quotas, where workers are pushed to the edge, collapsing from the pace.

This rush to meet expectations and deliver instantly affects our *health* and *well-being*.

Social Factors – *A Patience Trap*

Let's not exclude the education system: rewarding speed over depth as part of workplace culture.

The same *impatience* is mirrored in our education system. From an early age, we are taught to value *speed* over mastery. I remember my *exam days*—the emphasis was on quick answers, with no time to reflect or think deeply. As I *edit scripts*, I catch myself rushing to finish rather than taking the time to refine. It's a habit ingrained from years of being taught that the faster you complete something, the better you are at it.

My son faces similar pressures in *high school*. Every *deadline* feels like a race against time, with little room for deep thought. The pace is relentless, and the *patience* to truly explore topics is shrinking. This is where our education system often falls short.

A prominent educational thinker, John Dewey, argued that learning should foster *reflection* and *critical thinking*, not just haste.

Unfortunately, modern education systems, especially in many *Western countries*, prize *speed* and *efficiency* over depth of *understanding*.

But there's hope. Take *Finland's education system*, for example. Their approach is slower-paced, focusing on *quality* over *quantity*. Students aren't just taught to regurgitate information quickly—they're encouraged to take their time, think critically, and develop *patience*. The result? Higher-quality learning, *happier* students, and better long-term outcomes.

In the rush to meet *deadlines*, hit *targets*, and keep up with the pace of modern life, we often forget the value of *patience*. Whether at work, in *education*, or in personal life, taking the time to reflect, master skills, and allow things to unfold at their own pace can lead to more profound success, fewer mistakes, and greater *peace of mind*.

I Lack Patience

The real challenge is not just about managing *impatience*, but also about understanding the larger *social forces* that shape how we experience it. So, next time you are in a rush, take a breath. The key to success is to slow down and let things unfold at their own pace.

The Ticking Clock – *Relationship Dynamics*

Impatience can seriously strain the bonds between people, especially in relationships where patience is most needed. I'll admit, I've lost my cool a few times—snapping at my wife over a minor delay in tea—when she was just outside, calmly getting things ready. My son, on the other hand, constantly bombards me with impatient "new phone?" texts, sparking rows.

It's a pattern—he does not wait, and I don't either. But one day, I held off, listened to my wife, and we laughed about it. Sometimes, slowing down and listening can turn the tide.

A good friend of mine once nearly saw his marriage unravel. Impatient jabs over household chores were taking their toll. However, things turned around when they decided to pause, discuss the situation, and communicate more slowly. They're still together today, and their relationship is stronger for it. Sometimes, patience is the key to finding a way forward, especially when things are most tense.

Carl Rogers, the well-known psychologist, once said, "Real communication occurs… when we listen with understanding." It's a simple truth. *Patience* helps us build bridges, not walls.

Social Factors – *A Patience Trap*

Therefore, the pressure of impatience can disrupt communication in relationships, whether romantic, familial, or platonic. Impatience leads to miscommunication, snapped tempers, and unresolved grievances. I've seen it in my own life, and I've witnessed it in others, too. When we don't slow down, we miss essential cues and fail to hear each other honestly. But when we allow space for patience, we find the time to understand, empathise, and connect.

The impatience we often feel can also affect family dynamics. I've noticed this with my kids, especially when they do not want to wait for something or get frustrated over minor delays. I cannot help but think of how patience (or lack thereof) can affect the parent-child relationship. When we allow *impatience* to take over, it can lead to unnecessary conflict, and if left unchecked, it can even harm our trust and respect.

But here's the thing: patience can rebuild relationships. By allowing ourselves the time to communicate thoughtfully, whether with a partner, child, or friend, we can begin to repair and strengthen our connections. I've seen relationships thrive after individuals make a conscious effort to slow down and listen.

For example, one couple I know made it a point to pause before responding during arguments. Their relationship has grown because they now understand each other better and know that taking the time to answer thoughtfully matters more than reacting quickly.

In the end, *impatience* may seem like a minor frustration in the moment, but it can have a significant impact on the health of our relationships.

The question is: Are we willing to pause, reflect, and listen with patience? It's a skill that can save relationships and turn them into something more profound, substantial, and meaningful.

IMPATIENCE IN EVERYDAY LIFE

The daily grind—*traffic*, *queues*, or *tech issues*—constantly challenges our *patience*. Little irritations test us, but how we handle them can change our experience.

My Take: I've been stuck in *traffic* more times than I care to count—on my way to a book meet, watching the minutes tick by, my frustration growing. The horn becomes my outlet as if it'll speed things up. Then there's my son—his bus is late, and the world is ending. "It's always late!" he complains, and I can't help but notice how easily *impatience* creeps in. The *tech* side doesn't help either—*Wi-Fi* cutting out in the middle of an edit.

I'm itching to keep working, but the lag is unbearable. Meanwhile, he's on about his *phone* lagging with every app. I'm sure you've felt it too—the itch of *impatience* building up in these everyday moments.

Take *queuing*—we've all been there, haven't we? Standing at the checkout, watching the line crawl forward. The longer it takes, the more irritated we become. But then, I noticed something: a man in front of me took a deep breath, smiled at the cashier, and started a light conversation. By the time he left, he and the cashier were smiling. He had used that time to relax rather than letting *impatience* take over. It was a slight shift, but it made a huge difference.

Social Factors – *A Patience Trap*

Why let *impatience* ruin a dull task when you could turn it into a moment of peace?

Thoreau's words about *"quiet desperation"* come to mind. He spoke of how the rush of everyday life—the constant striving for *speed*—ultimately creates *frustration*. The *impatience* that builds in these moments of rushing through life becomes a subtle force that erodes our *peace*.

So, how do we cope with these frustrations? *Traffic*, for example, used to get my blood boiling, but I've learned to use it as an opportunity for calm. Whether listening to podcast music or taking a deep breath, I've started seeing it as a chance to reset. When waiting in queues, instead of getting agitated, I try to look around, engage in small talk, or pause and take a breath.

The same goes for *technology*—I've learned to step back when things go wrong. Sometimes, the best way to handle *tech glitches* is to give myself a moment away from the screen, returning with a fresh mindset. The *internet* will get back on track when it's ready.

Managing *impatience* is about adjusting expectations. Life doesn't always move at our pace; sometimes, we must accept that. Rather than fighting the slow moments, we can choose to embrace them. *Mindset* plays a key role—seeing *traffic* as an opportunity for reflection, *queues* as a moment for rest, or *tech* issues as a reminder of what we can't control.

Ultimately, the little moments—*such as traffic jams, queues, and tech problems—make up a significant portion* of our day. How we react to them shapes our *mental space*. By adjusting our expectations and cultivating *patience*, we can navigate these challenges with less *frustration* and more *peace*.

The Social Pulse

Societal expectations, cultural norms, peer pressure, and technology constantly push us to act faster and erode our patience. We live in a world that celebrates speed over depth, and often, we don't realise how these external forces shape our ability to wait, pause, and reflect.

My Take: Growing up in Metropolitan City, the culture of "getting on with it" has always driven me. It's ingrained in how we work, always racing to the next task and trying to finish things as quickly as possible. I rush to finish scripts, thinking I need to meet expectations immediately. My son shares the same mindset—he believes everything should be instant. Meanwhile, in places like Japan, the slow rituals of tea ceremonies and deliberate craftsmanship seem like a world apart from our fast-paced, get-it-done-now mentality. Have you ever felt that pressure to hurry just because that's the pace around you?

Cultural Norms – *Speed as a Social Creed.* Cultural norms significantly influence how we perceive time and productivity. *Max Weber's* concept of the "Protestant work ethic"—the idea that "time is money"—still resonates deeply in many cultures. For instance, America's 24/7 hustle culture is rooted in the belief that constant activity leads to success. Contrast this with Spain's *siestas*, where taking the time to rest is culturally accepted. In the UK, we've become accustomed to keeping moving and pushing forward without realising how much we've internalized the *need for speed*. Have you ever felt overwhelmed by the rush to keep up with a world that demands more and faster?

Peer Pressure – *The Herd's Haste.* Peer pressure has a way of making impatience contagious. I see it with my mates—they boast about the gigs they're landing or the speed at which they complete their work. Suddenly,

Social Factors – *A Patience Trap*

I must keep up and push my creative work faster to match their pace. My son is experiencing this too; he's constantly comparing himself to his friends, whether getting the latest tech or achieving something before anyone else. *Alain de Botton's* concept of "status anxiety" perfectly sums up this impatience—when we fall behind, we rush to catch up. Have you ever been speeding up to match someone else's pace?

Technology and Connectivity – *Instant Everything.* Technology has turned us into a generation of instant gratification seekers. My inbox is always open, and when it's empty, I get antsy, waiting for the next bit of feedback or communication. My son's obsession with his phone is no different; he's always expecting instant replies and quick fixes. The Samsung Note 7 disaster is a prime example of how impatience can lead to catastrophic failures—pushed out to compete, it ended in tragedy.

Neil Postman once said, "We are all 'enchanted' by the tools we create," and nowhere is this more apparent than in the rapid pace of technological advancements today. The tools we've created for connection have evolved faster than we can handle, creating a cycle of frustration when things don't go as quickly as expected. Have you ever felt the disappointment of a technology glitch or delay that tests your patience?

Urban Living – *The Restless Beat.* Urbanisation plays a massive part in how we manage impatience. The hustle of city life—crowded streets, heavy traffic, long commutes—creates a constant buzz of urgency. *Thoreau's* concept of "quiet desperation" feels even more poignant when you're stuck in a traffic jam, racing to a meeting that will never take place. My son often fumes when his bus is delayed, feeling the weight of that lost time. The city's constant demand for speed and efficiency exacerbates impatience, prompting us to be constantly 'on the go.' Have you ever felt that growing frustration from the city's pace?

Media Influence – *Urgency's Drumbeat.* The media promotes *speed* everywhere: instant deals, quick fixes, buy now, act now. I'm guilty of it, too—those ads push my books, giving me that sense of urgency to sell quickly. My son sees the same phone ads; before you know it, he's asking for the latest model. In a sense, the media is the *medium* through which this impatience spreads. *Marshall McLuhan* argued, "The medium is the message," and today's media constantly scream "speed" at us. Have you ever purchased something because of a flash sale or an urgent offer?

Economic Pressures – *Survival's Sprint.* Financial pressures are another significant factor contributing to impatience. The drive to make quick money has created a *culture of hustle* in the gig economy, where people feel pressured to work nonstop. I take on extra gigs, squeezing time for writing to make ends meet. Fresh out of school, my son wanted a credit card at 18, believing that instant access to cash would solve everything. *Max Weber's* theory on capitalism's emphasis on speed rings true—impatience often stems from the constant pressure to generate wealth quickly. Have you ever felt the need to *hustle* to survive?

Societal Expectations – *The Success Dash.* Ultimately, society's emphasis on success can foster impatience. Everything feels like a race, whether it's the pressure to finish that project or reach milestones in life. I constantly feel like I'm "behind" in my work, trying to keep up with the expectations of quick results. My son faces similar pressures, rushing towards adulthood and wanting instant access to adult privileges. *Alain de Botton* touches on this when he discusses the "myth of progress"—the belief that we should consistently achieve faster. Does it ever feel like you're sprinting to keep up, only to realise that it's not the race, but the journey, that matters?

SOCIAL FACTORS – *A Patience Trap*

Tying It Together – *Society's Shaping Hand.* From my father's hurried ways to my son's need for instant gratification, I see how *society* shapes our *impatience*. The relentless *hustle* at work, the pressure to keep up in the city, and the technology that quickens us to act contribute to our daily impatience. However, understanding this is power. Once we realise the external forces that drive us, we can start making conscious decisions to slow down, nurture *patience*, and reclaim control over how we move through life. *Where is society pulling your patience*? Let's recognise it and choose to be patient, step by step.

THE SOCIAL GETAWAY – *THE PATIENCE TOOLBOX*

Impatience can infiltrate our professional lives in many subtle ways. Whether waiting for a response to an important email, navigating through a busy workday, or dealing with a frustrating project delay, impatience can easily take hold and disrupt our professional interactions. However, there are simple, effective strategies that can help us manage impatience and develop stronger, more patient-professional relationships. Let's break down some practical exercises to guide you towards better patience in professional situations.

1. Recognising Impatience: *The First Step*

Before we can manage impatience, we must recognise when it arises. This powerful tool allows us to act proactively and avoid letting impatience control us, empowering us to take charge of our social interactions.

Exercise: *Impatience Tracker*

Keep a journal for a week. Track situations when you felt impatient—waiting for a message, a colleague's response, or a delayed train.

Write down what happened, how you felt, and how it impacted the interaction. Look for patterns at the end of the week: What triggered your impatience? Was it external pressure, or were you feeling rushed?

Example: If you feel impatient during meetings where others speak at length, consider whether your need to intervene causes frustration.

2. Empathy-Building Exercises: *Softening the Edge*

Empathy is a powerful antidote to impatience and a bridge connecting us to others. It is much easier to remain calm and patient when we understand where others are coming from.

Exercise: *Empathy Mapping*

Choose a person in your life—whether a colleague, friend, or family member—and imagine their perspective in a situation that frustrates you.

Create a map:

- What do they see?
- What are they feeling?
- What are they thinking?
- How are they reacting?

Example: Imagine a colleague missing a deadline. Instead of thinking they are careless, think about their workload, personal struggles, or lack of support. This can help you empathise and respond more patiently.

3. Active Listening: *Hearing Beyond the Hurry*

Active listening is not just a key strategy in managing impatience; it's a way to show respect and understanding. It ensures that we genuinely understand the other person before reacting. By actively listening, we're less likely to interrupt or become impatient, which fosters better communication and stronger relationships.

Exercise: *5-Minute Listening Challenge*

Here's a practical exercise that can significantly improve your listening skills and patience. Pair up with someone and engage in a 5-minute conversation. The challenge is to refrain from interrupting. Show your engagement by making eye contact, nodding, and paraphrasing what they say. Afterward, reflect on how you felt listening without rushing. This exercise can be a game-changer in your journey to manage impatience.

Example: Instead of preparing your response while someone else is talking in a meeting, focus entirely on their words. This prevents you from getting frustrated or cutting them off.

4. Imagining Others' Perspectives: *Stepping Outside*

Impatience often arises from a lack of understanding of why someone behaves a certain way. However, stepping outside our perspective and imagining theirs can reduce frustration and increase patience.

In this context, empathy is not just a tool; it's a powerful weapon in managing impatience. It enables us to see the situation from the other person's perspective, fostering understanding and patience.

Exercise: *Role Reversal*

Think of a situation where you felt frustrated with someone. Imagine you are in their shoes—what were they thinking, feeling, or experiencing? Write down your reflections.

Example: If a family member is always late, consider what might happen—perhaps they are overwhelmed with work or other responsibilities. Understanding their situation can help you be more patient.

5. Communication Stratagems: *Saying It Steady*

How we communicate plays a significant role in preventing impatience from escalating into conflict. By expressing ourselves calmly and assertively, we create an environment that fosters understanding and patience to flourish.

Exercise: *Assertive Patience*

In situations where impatience may arise, practise assertive communication by expressing your thoughts calmly. For instance, if someone is rushing you, say: "I need a moment to think this through. Let us revisit this in 10 minutes." This sets boundaries without aggression.

Example: When a friend repeats the same complaint, instead of getting impatient, you might say, "I can hear that this is important to you. Let us discuss this in more detail when I have the time to listen fully."

6. Practice Patience *in Small Doses*

Patience is a skill that strengthens with practice. The more you incorporate patience into your daily life, the more natural it becomes. This approach enables you to start small and gradually expand into more challenging situations, providing a sense of control and alleviating

Social Factors – *A Patience Trap*

overwhelming feelings. Practicing patience in small doses can make you feel more in control and less overwhelmed in difficult situations.

Exercise: *Daily Patience Challenge*

Daily, find at least one situation to practice patience—dealing with a delayed email, waiting in line, or managing a stressful conversation. Use one of the techniques you have learned, like active listening, empathy, or setting boundaries. This consistent practice of patience, even in small doses, can significantly impact how you handle challenging situations.

Example: Practice patience by listening to music or a podcast during your daily commute, rather than stressing over the delays.

Take a moment to breathe at work before responding to an email that has frustrated you.

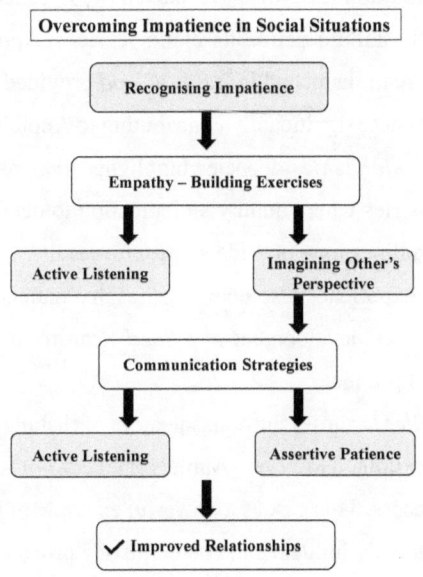

CASE STUDY: MOBILEME BY APPLE (2008)

In 2008, Apple launched MobileMe, a cloud-based service that syncs emails, contacts, and calendars across its devices. The project aimed to enhance the user experience by integrating Apple's ecosystem. However, due to the pressure to release MobileMe alongside the highly anticipated iPhone 3G, impatience led to a simultaneous launch that resulted in significant flaws.

The Problem: MobileMe was released with significant flaws in the rush to meet the iPhone 3 G deadline. The service experienced technical issues, including email disruptions, syncing errors, and lost contacts. These failures resulted from inadequate testing, as the team prioritised meeting the deadline over ensuring the product's quality. The impatience to launch quickly led to widespread user frustration and damaged Apple's reputation for reliability, highlighting the negative impact of impatience in professional settings.

Outcome: After the *MobileMe* failure, Apple publicly acknowledged the mistakes. Steve Jobs admitted that the launch was rushed and a "mistake." Instead of letting the failure define its cloud services, Apple used the lessons learned to create *iCloud*, launched in 2011. *iCloud* provided a more reliable and user-friendly experience, significantly contributing to Apple's continued success.

Learning: The *MobileMe* debacle highlights the risks of impatience, particularly in industries where quality and attention to detail are crucial. While rushing to meet deadlines may provide short-term results, it often leads to long-term setbacks. The experience also demonstrates that patience and refinement—like those shown in the development of *iCloud*—can result in a much stronger and more successful product.

Takeaway: *MobileMe* shows the consequences of rushing a product to market without adequate testing. However, Apple's success with *iCloud* proves that patience o great success. This case is a powerful example of how impatience and patience can dramatically influence the outcome of a project.

6.
MINDSET SHIFT – *Reframing Our Lenses*

"Patience is not simply the ability to wait - it's how we behave while we're waiting." - John Ortberg.

Impatience is that restless, twitchy feeling when the world does not seem to move fast enough for you. It is a very human experience, and history is full of fascinating stories of what happens when *impatience* is left unchecked—and when we use it as a catalyst for something better. One such example comes from *Winston Churchill* during World War II. As Britain faced adversity, Churchill's leadership required both *impatience* for victory and the *patience* to endure long, arduous years of struggle.

Despite the slow progress, he remained steadfast, constantly reminding the British people, *"Success is not final, failure is not fatal: It is the courage to continue that counts."* His ability to stay committed to the long-term goal despite the immense challenges shows how *impatience* for success must be balanced with the *patience* to face setbacks. This balance is a guiding principle that reassures us that we can navigate the challenges of impatience.

I Lack Patience

This *impatience* often stems from our *mindset*—how we perceive time, react to obstacles, and respond to delays. *Shifting* from *impatience* to *patience* is not just a nice idea—it's a necessary skill for navigating today's fast-paced world. The *first step* in this shift is realising that we have the power to change how we respond to delays. This power is in our hands and a tool we can use to navigate the challenges of our fast-paced world.

During the pandemic's peak in 2020, many people were forced to adjust to long waits for essentials like groceries or vaccines. Instead of giving in to frustration, some used this time to reflect, reconnect with loved ones, or even pick up new hobbies. This *patience* in the face of disruption helped many shift their perspective, turning delays into opportunities for personal growth.

To cultivate this kind of patience, practise mindfulness, engage in activities that bring joy, or remind yourself that the delay is not the end of the journey but a part of it. It is a reminder that, like *Churchill*'s wartime leadership, we can use setbacks as chances to build strength and resilience.

In moments of *impatience*, we feel like time is slipping away, but in reality, we often rush toward outcomes that might not bring lasting peace.

A Mindful Turn

One powerful tool for shifting our mindset is *mindfulness*. Steve Jobs, co-founder of Apple, was known for his calm approach to challenges. He often spoke about staying present and focused on the task. When faced with problems, Jobs didn't rush to find a solution. Instead, he took a step back, pausing to assess every detail of the situation, embodying *mindfulness* and giving his mind the space to work through the complexity.

At its core, *mindfulness* is about being fully present in the moment—observing our thoughts and feelings without judgment. Whether stuck in traffic or waiting for a colleague's reply, we can pause and check in with ourselves instead of giving in to impatience.

Are we feeling tense? Is our heart racing? Are we mentally rushing ahead, thinking about what to do when we are "free"? This self-awareness is the first step in regaining control. By acknowledging our impatience without judgment, we free ourselves from its grip and create space for *patience* to emerge naturally.

The Power of Small Shifts

Shifting from *impatience* to *patience* is not an instant transformation. It's a gradual journey that begins with recognizing our *impatience*, acknowledging it, and then making a conscious decision to respond differently.

This choice is not just a change in behaviour; it's a powerful act of self-empowerment. It demonstrates that we are the masters of our reactions. Consider a seasoned *mountain climber*.

They encounter numerous challenges on their way to the summit. Instead of rushing or succumbing to frustration, they carefully evaluate each step, plan their moves, and pace themselves, using the time to reflect on their journey. Over time, these small shifts in approach enable them to reach the peak with a calm mind and steady hand.

I Lack Patience

As these small shifts accumulate, we develop a new habit of *patience*. Instead of being at the mercy of our emotions and reactions, we learn to manage them, fostering a more harmonious, tranquil life. This tranquillity, born from a life *of* balance and patience, is a serene state of existence within everyone's reach.

We all have the potential to nurture *patience*, but it begins with a *certain mindset*. It's about understanding that we can't control everything around us, but we can control our responses.

By embracing *mindfulness*, practising *self-compassion*, and adjusting our perception of time, we can transition from *impatience* to *patience* in our actions and hearts.

In a world that's always in a hurry, choosing *patience* is one of the most empowering things we can do for ourselves and those around us. So, the next time impatience starts *to* creep in, take a moment, breathe, and remember that sometimes, the best thing you can do is wait.

Self-Compassion – Being Kind to Ourselves

Another key element in shifting from *impatience* to *patience* is *self-compassion*. It's easy to get frustrated with ourselves when we feel rushed and feel as if we should be doing things faster or more efficiently. Take *Oprah Winfrey*, who has spoken about the challenges she faced early in her career.

Despite numerous setbacks, from being fired from her first job in television to facing a public backlash, Oprah learned to treat herself with kindness. Instead of harshly judging herself for "not being good enough,"

Mindset Shift – *Reframing Our Lenses*

she embraced *self-compassion*, which allowed her to continue growing and ultimately achieve immense success.

Self-compassion reminds us that we are human and can make mistakes, experience delays, and face challenges. When we are impatient, instead of berating ourselves, we can pause and say, *"It's okay. This is just a moment. I am learning, and I'll do better next time."*

This simple act of kindness towards ourselves can instantly shift our *mindset*, reducing frustration and replacing it with *patience*.

Changing Our Perspective on Time

A considerable part of shifting from *impatience* to *patience* is changing our perspective on time itself. In today's world, we have been conditioned to think that speed equals success. We are often told to "hurry up," "get it done fast," and "keep moving." But the reality is that *patience* is not about sitting idle and waiting for things to happen—it is about recognising that some of the best things in life take time.

Take *a student* preparing for exams who might feel impatient about the results. Instead of focusing on the outcome, they can learn to enjoy the process of learning and growth. This shift in perspective can help them develop patience and reduce stress.

When we change our perspective and see delays not as obstacles but as opportunities to slow down, reflect, or even enjoy the moment, we open ourselves up to a more peaceful way of being.

Instead of seeing time as something "wasted," we can shift our focus to what can be gained at that moment—whether it's a moment of rest, a chance to think, or the opportunity to connect with those around us.

I Lack Patience

Mind Over Matter

I have rushed through tasks, driven by *ego*, thinking I was the fastest, only to end with sloppy work. My impatience was not just about waiting in lines or the busy buzz around me; it came from how I saw myself and reacted to challenges. *Ego*, *attitude*, and *impulses* play a big part, all tangled with *status* and *setbacks*. Take the 1986 *Challenger* disaster—NASA's pride led them to ignore warnings, causing a fatal mistake. It reminds me of how impatience can lead to poor decisions, like when I rushed through scripts. My mindset is personal, but it is not fixed, and I am learning to shift mine, which has made everything from work to traffic jams more manageable.

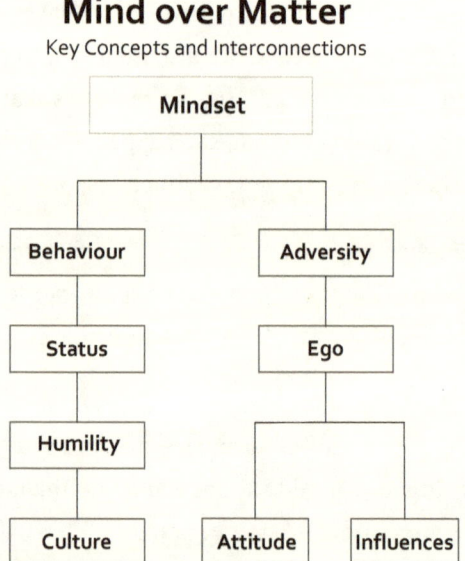

Mind over Matter
Key Concepts and Interconnections

MINDSET SHIFT – *Reframing Our Lenses*

Ego, driven by *pride*, convinces us that being the fastest or the best defines us, pushing us to rush through tasks, miss details, and end up frustrated with sloppy work. I've experienced this when I ran through scripts thinking I was quicker than everyone else, only to realise I missed glaring mistakes. But when I shifted my mindset to focus on *progress* over *perfection*, I started allowing myself time to breathe and reflect, and my work improved. *Viktor Frankl* once said, "What is to give light must endure burning," reminding us that enduring challenges with *patience* can lead to better outcomes.

Attitude is crucial in how we handle impatience. I used to get frustrated with delayed replies, thinking people were slacking, but changing my perspective to "They are probably busy" relieved me. *Humility* helps avoid snap judgments, and adopting it brings more patience. We are all driven by *impulse*—to act quickly or rush—but that only adds stress. A prime example is the 2010 *Flash Crash*, where impulsive decisions caused a massive market drop in minutes. By pausing, I've learned to slow down and make better decisions.

Our *behaviour* shapes our *mindset*. I used to work late, rushing everything and feeling stressed, but focusing on one task at a time helped improve my work and calm my mind. *Steve Wozniak*, co-founder of Apple, took his time to get things right, showing that patience pays off. I'm trying to break the "busy" habit by taking breaks—like walking instead of scrolling—which has dramatically impacted my *mindset*.

Status often fuels impatience. I would see others getting ahead and feel like I was falling behind, pushing harder but making more mistakes. I realised chasing *status* is a trap. I started celebrating small wins—like writing one solid page—rather than obsessing over becoming a bestseller. *This shift in focus towards celebrating small victories has been*

I Lack Patience

encouraging, reminding me that progress is made one step at a time. Enron is an excellent example of how chasing *status* can lead to disaster. True *patience* comes when we stop trying to keep up and focus on what truly matters.

Adversity tests our patience. Setbacks, like rejection, are opportunities to pause and reflect. *Malala Yousafzai* showed incredible patience when she continued her studies despite facing threats from the Taliban (Yousafzai, 2013). *Adversity* can teach us if we let it.

The **influences** around us—whether from *friends*, *social media*, or *culture*—can either speed us up us up or slow us down. I used to feel pressured to hustle harder, but by unfollowing the noise and focusing on calming influences, I have shifted my *mindset* to one of balance.

Culture may set the pace, but it does not dictate it. I've seen that *patience* exists in both fast-paced cities and the slower rhythm of places like *Japan*, just at different speeds.

Shifting our **mindset** is not easy, but we can create space between stimulus and response by changing our *attitude*, controlling our *impulses*, and focusing on personal growth rather than chasing *status*. This shift in focus gives us a sense of control over our lives, allowing us to move towards a calmer, more *patient* version of ourselves, ready to face life's challenges with steadier, more grounded energy.

Waiting vs Waiting Patiently

I used to think that *waiting* was just another word for *patience*, or at least something close to it—like a half-baked cake that was almost there but

Mindset Shift – *Reframing Our Lenses*

not entirely. It seemed to balance how we handle situations, and I'd call it things like *maturity* or *understanding*. But I never realised that waiting, in its true sense, is often entirely *passive*—and it can quickly lead to *frustration* or even an *urge* to explode.

Waiting feels like something controlled by external forces, where you have little or no control over the outcome—like waiting for a *train* to arrive on time. It's the kind of thing that often triggers *impatience*, that itch to act or *win*. I'd catch myself stewing over a late email, muttering, "Come on, reply!"—as if my stare could somehow make it happen faster. *Waiting* is tied to *passivity*, often dictated by the *circumstances* around us, and it can feel like you're doing nothing while time ticks by.

While *waiting* can be frustrating and unproductive, psychologist *Kurt Lewin* pointed out that *it* is a dynamic process, with each individual reacting to it based on their *emotions* and *expectations*. When you feel you have no control over the situation, you slip into passive waiting, and that's when *frustration*, *anxiety*, and even *resentment* creep in.

Take waiting for a delayed *flight*, for instance—when there's no information or action you can take, it's easy to feel irritated. This *waiting* can drain your *energy* and create negative emotional states.

Conversely, *active waiting* or *waiting patiently* is about controlling your *emotions* and *actions*. It's about shifting your perspective and reframing the situation to align with your *values* and *purpose*. Instead of passively sitting there, you can use the time to do something constructive, like *learning* or *reflecting*. In simpler terms, it's about making the most of your time while waiting, rather than letting the wait frustrate you. This kind of waiting is much more challenging, but ultimately, it's a much

I Lack Patience

more *positive* experience that leads to *personal growth* and a greater sense of *fulfilment*.

Waiting is something we all experience, whether it's waiting for a *bus*, a *job offer*, or even a more significant change in the world. But there's a fundamental difference between simply *waiting* and *waiting patiently*. Both involve the passage of *time*, but the *approach* and *mental state* are entirely different.

Waiting patiently involves deliberately deciding to delay *action* and giving yourself space for *strategic planning*, *reflection*, and *timing*. *Waiting patiently* often leads to better outcomes, more thoughtful *decision-making*, and a better chance of success. It's not passive at all—it's an *active* mindset that embraces delay rather than resisting it.

Take *Apollo 13*, for example, when NASA's team had to wait as oxygen was running low, yet their calm and steady planning—keeping their heads cool for hours—ultimately saved the astronauts. *Patience* transforms *waiting* into time for *thinking*, *growth*, and *peace*.

William James, another psychologist, talked about the difference between passive waiting, which often leads to *frustration*, and active waiting, which builds *resilience*.

Active waiting is about focusing on what can be *controlled* while you wait, whether preparing for a future task, *learning* something new, or taking small steps towards bigger goals.

On the other hand, passive *waiting* can lead to *impatience*, *restlessness*, and *mental exhaustion*, as we experience when waiting in long queues or stuck in traffic. The *mind* gets overwhelmed, which impacts both *emotional* and *physical health*.

Mindset Shift – *Reframing Our Lenses*

Mindset vs. Reaction

When we talk about *patience*, it's easy to focus on the outward actions—how we behave while *waiting*, how long we can endure something, or how we manage our reactions. However, what often gets overlooked is the *mindset* we bring to these moments and how it shapes our *reactions*. Our mindset can determine whether we experience *peace* or *frustration* during *waiting*. It's not just about how long we can tolerate something, but how we engage mentally with the situation.

The key difference between *mindset* and *reaction* is that while *mindset* is *internal*, *reaction* is *external*. Our *mindset* sets the stage for how we experience *waiting* and interpret the time spent. Our *reaction*, in turn, directly results from this internal state and reveals how we engage with others and the situation.

For instance, if a *customer service* agent is rude, your *mindset* might help you see the agent as having a bad day rather than taking their behaviour personally. This *mindset* results in a *calm*, collected *reaction*, where you maintain your *composure* rather than lashing out. However, suppose you adopt a more negative *mindset*. In that case, they're out to get me," or "This is a waste of my time"—your *reaction* could involve *frustration* or *anger*, escalating the situation unnecessarily.

Mindset is the internal lens through which we interpret the world around us. It influences how we perceive challenges, setbacks, and delays. For example, a *growth-oriented mindset* might see a long wait as an opportunity to reflect, relax, or even work on a personal goal. On the other hand, someone with a *negative* or *fixed mindset* might view the same situation as an obstacle or a waste of time, leading to *frustration*. Peace here refers to calm and acceptance, even amid delays or challenges.

I Lack Patience

Consider *waiting* for a *job offer*. A person with a *growth-oriented mindset* might see this as a chance to sharpen their skills, look for other opportunities, or work on *self-improvement*. This mindset helps make the wait more bearable and makes the most of the time. Conversely, someone with a *fixed mindset* might focus only on the *anxiety* of *waiting*, seeing it as a *punishment* or failure, thereby missing out on potential growth opportunities.

Mindset is what allows us to *reframe* the *waiting* process. It transforms a frustrating, passive experience into something meaningful. Reframing here means changing the way we view the situation. When we shift our *perspective* from helplessness to *openness* or *opportunity*, we can change how we experience *patience*.

Reaction, on the other hand, is the outward expression of our *thoughts* and *emotions*. It's what happens when the *waiting* period ends or when the pressure of the wait becomes overwhelming. Our *reaction* is often the first sign of how well we've managed our *mindset* during the wait.

For example, imagine waiting for hours at the *doctor's office*. Your *reaction* could range from *frustration* and *anger* to *acceptance* and *calmness*. If your *response* is *impatience*, your body tenses up, and your mind races, making the wait feel unbearably long. However, if your *mindset* is rooted in *patience*, you might accept the wait, breathe deeply, and perhaps use the time to read a book or plan your day.

What is crucial here is that *reactions* stem from *mindset*. Our outward *reactions*—whether snapping at someone, tapping our foot *impatiently*, or sighing loudly—are often influenced by how we think about the situation. We're more likely to react negatively if we view the *wait* as challenging.

MINDSET SHIFT – *Reframing Our Lenses*

However, if we see it as an opportunity to rest or regroup, we can approach it peacefully, thereby taking control of our emotional responses.

UNDERSTANDING GROWTH MINDSET

As Carol Dweck explained, a growth mindset is the belief that abilities and intelligence can be developed over time through *effort, learning*, and persistence. This mindset is crucial because it fosters *resilience* and allows us to approach challenges positively, seeing them as opportunities to improve rather than obstacles.

People with a *growth mindset* believe they can always learn, adapt, and improve even if they face difficulties or fail. On the other hand, a *fixed mindset* sees abilities as static and unchangeable, which leads to a *fear of failure, impatience*, and a reluctance to take on challenges. Those with a *fixed mindset* often avoid difficulties because they fear not succeeding, limiting their growth potential. By adopting a growth mindset, individuals can unlock their full potential, learn from their experiences, and ultimately achieve tremendous success in their personal and professional lives.

Patience, a cornerstone of *a growth mindset*, provides a sense of *calm* and reassurance in the face of setbacks. *It* allows us to take our time, reflect on what went wrong, and find ways to improve rather than rushing to fix things or give up. *Patience* teaches us that growth is a journey, not a destination—it takes time and effort.

In contrast, a *fixed mindset* makes us focus on quick results and perfection, which leads to frustration and a fear of making mistakes. When things don't go as planned, people with a *fixed mindset* are more likely to give up or feel defeated, while those with a *growth mindset* are motivated to keep going, knowing that every mistake is an opportunity to learn and grow.

In practice, a *growth mindset* encourages us to embrace challenges with curiosity and determination. Instead of seeing setbacks as failures, we see them as stepping stones towards improvement. For example, in academics, a person with a *growth mindset* might view a low grade as an opportunity to learn and improve, while someone with a fixed mindset might see it as a reflection of their intelligence.

Similarly, in sports, a *growth mindset* might lead a player to see a loss as a chance to identify weaknesses and improve, while a fixed mindset might lead to feelings of defeat. In these situations, *patience* is essential in *a growth mindset* because it allows us to stay focused on the bigger picture, understanding that success is a process that takes time and persistence. By cultivating *patience*, we can remain calm, reflect on our experiences, and continue moving forward, knowing that every challenge we face is part of our journey to improvement and success.

REFRAMING PATIENCE AS A STRENGTH

Patience is often misunderstood as a passive act of simply waiting for something to happen. Still, when we reframe it as an *active skill*, it becomes a powerful tool for managing our *emotions*, responding thoughtfully, and navigating challenges, as it enables us to remain focused on long-term goals rather than being overwhelmed by immediate setbacks, allowing us to choose how we react and engage with the process meaningfully.

This perspective aligns with *Angela Duckworth*, a renowned psychologist known for her research on *grit*, which emphasises that perseverance and passion for long-term goals are key to success. Duckworth argues that success is not just about talent but the ability to persist through difficulties with patience, making it a central part of achieving our goals. By seeing *patience* as an active force, we gain the *resilience* to face obstacles with determination and the ability to make thoughtful decisions, knowing that true *success* often requires enduring challenges and delays, which in turn fosters *growth* over time, much like how *Albert Einstein* once said, "It's not that I'm so smart, it's just that I stay with problems longer." This highlights the importance of persistence, which is deeply connected to *patience*.

Patience is essential in *long-term planning*, *innovation*, and *problem-solving*, as it allows us to pursue our goals consistently, even when progress is slow, and enables us to take the time to reflect, adjust, and improve, ensuring that we make better decisions and ultimately achieve lasting success. For example, Thomas Edison's *patience* was a key factor in his development of the electric light bulb, as he failed countless times before succeeding, famously stating, "I have not failed. I've just found 10,000 ways that won't work." Edison's journey is a testament to how *patience* in the face of failure can lead to groundbreaking success. Similarly, *patience* is integral to creative problem-solving, where allowing ourselves time to reflect and iterate ultimately results in more innovative and effective solutions.

Moreover, *patience* is closely tied to *self-discipline*, a core component of *emotional intelligence*, as it allows us to regulate our impulses, resist frustration, and make measured, thoughtful choices, strengthening our ability to remain calm and focused under pressure, leading to better decision-making.

I Lack Patience

Daniel Goleman, a renowned psychologist and the author of *Emotional Intelligence*, argues that *self-control*—a key aspect of emotional intelligence—is rooted in patience, as it involves managing our reactions to stress, disappointment, and obstacles. The connection between *patience* and *self-control* enables us to focus on long-term goals, even when immediate gratification is tempting, helping us make decisions that align with our values.

Embracing *patience* as a strength and recognising its connection to *self-control* and *emotional intelligence*, we develop the capacity to manage challenges gracefully and focus on long-term aspirations.

The Science Behind Patience and Success

The science behind *patience* shows that it is not just about waiting—it is about how practising *patience* helps our brains handle stress, focus better, and make better decisions. When we are patient, we activate the *prefrontal cortex*, the part of the brain responsible for controlling our *emotions*, *planning*, and *impulses*. This helps us resist the urge for instant gratification and focus on long-term rewards, improving our problem-solving ability.

For example, when waiting for a big decision or project to complete, our *patience* helps us stay calm, leading to better decision-making. Additionally, practising *patience* reduces *stress* by lowering the amount of *cortisol*, the stress hormone, while increasing *dopamine* and *oxytocin*, which make us feel good and help us stay positive even when things aren't going fast. For instance, a person waiting to hear back from a job interview might feel anxious, but practising *patience* allows them to stay

Mindset Shift – *Reframing Our Lenses*

calm and wait for the outcome without getting overly stressed. The long-term benefits of patience give us hope and optimism for the future.

Patience also has significant *psychological benefits*. It helps boost *self-esteem*, as we feel more confident when we can stay calm and not give up easily. For example, someone trying to lose weight may face setbacks, but being patient with the process and not expecting immediate results helps them stay positive and keep going.

Patience can also reduce *anxiety* because it teaches us to accept delays and uncertainties rather than worrying about what might happen next. Instead of getting upset over a long queue, a person practising *patience* can use the time to relax or think rather than stress about it.

In various life situations, such as waiting for a promotion, dealing with a difficult colleague, or managing a challenging project, patience can be a powerful tool for maintaining composure and making better decisions.

Finally, *patience* plays a crucial role in improving our *relationships* with others. For instance, if you disagree with a friend or colleague, practising patience means listening to their point of view without interrupting or reacting too quickly. This helps build trust and understanding and fosters more substantial and positive relationships. In the end, *patience* is a valuable skill that helps us manage *stress*, improve *focus*, and strengthen *relationships*, ultimately leading to tremendous *success*.

Case Study:
Thomas Edison and the Invention of the Light Bulb

Thomas Edison's journey to invent the electric light bulb exemplifies the power of patience. His path was marked not by instant success but by countless failures, experiments, and determination. Edison's patience amid repeated setbacks is especially striking—he spent years testing thousands of materials to find the ideal filament. Each failure was not a defeat but an opportunity to learn, propelling him forward rather than discouraging him.

His famous remark, "I've not failed; I've just found 10,000 ways that won't work," encapsulates his mindset. Edison saw failure not as an endpoint but a necessary step toward success. His commitment to the process—refining methods, learning from mistakes, and staying focused—highlights that patience is not a passive state, but an active engagement in pursuing a long-term goal.

Edison's context makes his achievement even more impressive. He did not succumb to frustration or rush the process without assurance that his invention would work or be commercially viable. Instead, he maintained meticulous attention to detail and a deep commitment to innovation. His persistence ultimately led to the creation the first commercially viable light bulb, a revolutionary invention that transformed how people live and work, and continues to illuminate our world today.

This case illustrates the importance of patience, persistence, and faith in one's vision for driving meaningful innovation. Edison's story reminds us that true success often stems from sustained effort. It's not about quick wins, but about enduring difficulties, embracing iteration, and remaining committed to progress. Doing so becomes a powerful force for overcoming obstacles and realizing extraordinary goals.

7.
A WORLD IN A HURRY – *A New Normal*

"Impatience is the enemy of progress." - Unknown

Throughout history, humans have always found ways to make life more convenient. Take the first *wheel*, for example—this simple invention changed how we moved from walking to riding horses, eventually leading to *locomotives*, *trains*, and *planes*. Each of these innovations made time more valuable, and slowly, *patience* started to take a backseat. However, it wasn't until the late 20th century that the pace of change began to accelerate. In the 1960s, the *internet* was born, thanks to the pioneering work of Paul Baran and Donald Davies in the United States and the United Kingdom, who laid the groundwork for what we now know as the internet. This new technology completely altered our perception of time. Suddenly, everything needed to happen at lightning speed. Information became instantly accessible, and patience was no longer the virtue it once was. We put impatience in the *driver's seat*, and everything started accelerating.

I Lack Patience

Fast forward to today, and we have *AI*—a technology that has complicated our lives in ways we didn't anticipate. Sure, it makes some tasks more manageable, but it's also created a rush and an expectation that everything must happen instantly. For instance, AI-powered customer service chatbots are expected to respond within seconds, and AI-driven search engines provide results in milliseconds. It's as if education helped us evolve beyond thumb impressions, but now technology has made us regress, asking us if we're robots to enter an application or a website. It's almost as though we've gone full circle in some respects, and patience has become something we struggle with rather than embrace.

Contrastingly, during the 1940 *Dunkirk evacuation*, patience was not just a virtue but a necessity. Amid the chaos of *World War II*, when *German troops had cornered Allied forces*, a remarkable display of planning and perseverance unfolded. Over 338,000 soldiers were rescued from the beaches of *Dunkirk between 26 May and 4 June 1940*. This operation, known as *Operation Dynamo*, was not just a military maneuver but a testament to human resilience and strategic patience —a symphony of planning and execution in the face of overwhelming odds.

The planning was *meticulous*. The Allies had to devise a strategy that could overcome the challenges posed by the German forces and the geographical constraints of the Dunkirk area. The weather played a crucial role; the tides and winds were unpredictable, requiring precise timing and coordination. The use of tiny civilian boats, known as the *Little Ships*, was a stroke of genius. These vessels could navigate the shallow waters of the beaches, ferrying soldiers to larger ships waiting offshore. This ingenuity allowed the evacuation to proceed efficiently, even under constant threat from German aircraft and naval forces.

Deception was another critical element. The Allies employed various tactics to mislead the Germans about the scale and nature of the evacuation. These included feigned military activities and misinformation campaigns aimed at diverting enemy attention and resources away from Dunkirk. The patience to execute these strategies over an extended period while maintaining secrecy and morale was vital to the operation's success, adding a layer of tension and drama to the already high-stakes situation.

The Dunkirk evacuation was a remarkable lesson in modern *warfare*. It demonstrated that careful planning, strategic patience, and the willingness to adapt can lead to extraordinary outcomes despite overwhelming odds. It serves as a poignant reminder that in a world that often favours speed, there is still immense value in thinking, planning, and acting with *deliberation*, which is frequently overlooked in our fast-paced society.

THE EROSION OF PATIENCE IN MODERN SOCIETY

Companies like *Amazon*, *Zomato*, and other app-based service businesses have built their entire models around delivering goods or food in record or less time—often within 30 minutes. This not only caters to modern demands but also underscores the societal pressure for instant gratification. Customers now expect instant fulfilment, and any delay—even a minor one—can lead to frustration and complaints.

However, this impatience doesn't just affect consumers. The pressure on workers—whether *delivery drivers* or *warehouse staff*—raises serious *ethical concerns*. Employees are often forced to work at unsustainable speeds, risking their safety to meet tight deadlines. This creates a cycle where *societal impatience* not only shapes *consumer behaviour* but also leads to *systemic challenges* in industries prioritising speed over *well-being*. This is a societal issue that affects us all.

Once a cornerstone of human interaction and progress, patience has gradually slipped into the background, overshadowed by the relentless march of technological advancements and our increasing demand for instant gratification. Today, waiting is often viewed as an inconvenience, and we've been conditioned to believe that *instant gratification* is the norm. This loss of patience is not just a personal issue but a societal concern we must be aware of and address.

Take, for example, the evolution of *communication*. In the past, sending a letter could take days or even weeks to reach its destination. Now, we send instant messages that connect us with people worldwide in seconds.

We've traded *patience* for *speed*, and this shift extends to almost every part of life—*shopping*, *news*, or *entertainment*. In a world that demands everything to be immediate, *patience* feels like a concept from a bygone era. For instance, the rise of fast fashion and same-day delivery services has made waiting for a new outfit or a package a thing of the past. Even in entertainment, binge-watching TV shows has become the norm, eliminating the anticipation that comes with waiting for the next episode to air.

Philosopher Hartmut Rosa discusses this phenomenon in his theory of *social acceleration*. He argues that the rapid pace of *technological* and *social change* has compressed our sense of *time*, making everything feel rushed and hurried. We're always moving forward at breakneck speed, but paradoxically, *Rosa* calls this a *"frenetic standstill"*—a state where, despite all the acceleration, we're not getting any closer to true fulfilment. This means that while we're constantly busy and moving, we're not necessarily achieving a more profound sense of satisfaction or contentment.

We've been conditioned to believe that faster is always better, which has diminished our ability to appreciate the value of *delayed gratification* and the *enduring effort* required for long-term success. It's time we reflect on the importance of valuing patience and delayed gratification.

1. Technological Acceleration + Culture Shift

Technological advancements in the 21st century have significantly altered our expectations of *time* and *efficiency*. The advent of the *Internet*, *smartphones*, and *instant messaging* has cultivated an environment where *immediate gratification* is the norm. Studies indicate that users often abandon websites if they don't load within a few seconds, highlighting the diminished tolerance for *delays*.

This shift is not merely a reflection of *convenience* but also a *cultural transformation*. Historically, *communication* and *travel* required *patience*. Letters took weeks to reach their destinations, and journeys by sea spanned months. Today, a message can traverse the globe in seconds, and one can fly across continents in hours. This acceleration has reshaped our perception of *time* and, consequently, our ability to be patient.

Philosopher *Marshall McLuhan*'s concept of the *"global village"* anticipated this interconnectedness, where *technological advancements* compress *time* and *space*. However, this compression has led to what economist *Andrew Haldane* describes as an *"attention deficit disorder economy,"* where the rapid pace of *information flow* diminishes our ability to focus and delay *gratification*.

I Lack Patience

Modern *media* often glorify *"overnight"* successes, overshadowing the years of hard work that typically underlie such achievements. This narrative fosters unrealistic expectations and *impatience* in individuals. For instance, the rise of *social media influencers* who rapidly amass large followings can create a perception that success is quick and effortless. Such portrayals can diminish appreciation for the gradual achievement process and a heightened desire for *immediate results*.

Sociologist *Richard D. Lewis*, in his work *"When Cultures Collide,"* discusses how *cultural narratives* shape our *values* and *behaviours*. He notes that *cultures* emphasising *individualism* and *rapid success* contribute to societal *impatience*, where the *journey* is undervalued in favour of quick outcomes.

The rapid pace of *technological advancements* and the *cultural emphasis* on *immediate success* have eroded *patience* in modern society. As we continue to embrace *innovation*, we must recognise the value of *patience* and the processes that lead to meaningful achievements.

Philosopher *Bertrand Russell* stated, *"The time you enjoy wasting is not wasted."* In a world that often prioritises speed, taking the time to reflect and appreciate the *journey* can lead to more fulfilling and thoughtful outcomes.

Technological Acceleration + Culture Shift = Eroded Patience

2. Social Pressure + Cult of Instant Gratification

Social pressure is a deceitful web, often woven among *teenagers* and *young adults*. It can stem from anything and everything—peer influence, societal expectations, or the desire to conform to certain norms. Combined with the growing obsession with *instant gratification*, this pressure forms a potent cycle that fuels *impatience*.

Together, these forces shape *behaviours*, *decision-making*, and *self-worth*, often pushing individuals to seek *quick results* at the expense of *long-term satisfaction* and *perseverance*.

In a world where instant rewards are glorified, the ability to value sustained effort over immediate gratification has become increasingly rare, making recognising and challenging this cycle all the more critical.

How Social Pressure Fuels Instant Gratification -

Social pressure—the influence exerted by *peers, family*, and *society*—encourages individuals to conform to shared norms and expectations. In the context of *instant gratification*, this pressure manifests in several ways:

Social Media Validation: Platforms like *Instagram* and *TikTok* amplify the desire for *instant likes, comments*, and *shares*, pushing people to seek immediate *validation* and engage impulsively online.

FOMO (Fear of Missing Out): Watching others achieve *milestones, travel*, or experience *luxuries* in real time compels individuals to emulate these experiences, often without considering the consequences.

I Lack Patience

Achievement Culture: The constant race to *succeed*—whether in *education*, *career*, or *relationships*—discourages *patience*, fostering a mindset prioritising *immediate results* over sustained effort.

The Cult of Instant Gratification -

This *"cult"* operates almost like a belief system, where *instant rewards* are idolised, and *delayed gratification* is seen as outdated. Key aspects of this culture include:

Materialism: Consumer culture thrives on *instant purchases*, advertised as *"buy now, enjoy immediately."*

Short-Term Goals: The pursuit of *quick wins* overshadows the value of *long-term perseverance* and more profound satisfaction.

Addictive Technology: Apps, *games*, and *platforms* are designed with *dopamine*-triggering mechanisms that create dependency on *instant rewards*.

Breaking the Cycle -

Escaping the grip of *social pressure* and the *cult of instant gratification* requires a shift in *mindset* and conscious effort:

Practising Mindfulness: Developing awareness of *impulsive habits* can help individuals focus on meaningful actions rather than succumbing to *social pressures*.

Redefining Success: Shifting the narrative from *"faster is better"* to appreciating *slow, steady growth* can nurture *patience* and *resilience*.

Prioritising Offline Connections: Fostering *authentic relationships* outside the *digital realm* helps reduce the reliance on *online validation*.

We need to recognise the intertwined effects of *social pressure* and the allure of *instant gratification*. By taking small but meaningful steps, we can work toward a more balanced and fulfilling life. Ultimately, some of the best things in life are worth the wait. This understanding can inspire us to reassess our priorities and make adjustments that promote our overall well-being.

What do you think—can this cycle be effectively challenged?

> **Social Pressure + Cult of Instant Gratification = Forceful Cycle of Impatience**

3. Psychological and Societal Impacts

The decline of *patience* in today's world, as evidenced by [specific statistics or studies], is closely tied to *psychological* shifts and changes in society's functions. These influences have significantly altered how we perceive time, approach challenges, and pursue rewards, influencing our behavior both individually and collectively.

Stress and Mental Health

Impatience and *stress* are partners in crime. The more impatient we are, the more stress we seem to have, and that stress can lead to all sorts of *mental health problems*. We're constantly rushing to achieve *immediate results*, but this nonstop drive leaves little time to breathe and process our feelings. The pressure to continually perform keeps building, but if we never slow down, we end up mentally drained, unable to manage the stress that's piling up.

Example: Work Stress and Burnout

Think about someone in the office constantly being asked to meet tight deadlines, but there's no time to chill or recharge. The nonstop pressure to deliver quickly without taking a break can lead to burnout. The person gets so mentally drained that, despite trying hard, they can't perform at their best. When impatience takes over, we end up running ourselves into the ground, paying for it in terms of *mental health* and *productivity*.

Economic Consequences

In our society, where everyone chases *instant gratification*, impatience is also a big deal regarding *economic* issues. However, by choosing careful planning over quick results, we can avoid serious long-term problems and gain control over our financial stability.

Example: Impulsive Financial Decisions

Take the example of someone who invests in stocks, but instead of doing the research, they jump in because they see a quick trend and think they'll make a fast buck. This impatience for *quick financial returns* often leads to taking significant risks. Without considering the *investment's long-term stability, they incur a loss*. Another example could be someone who makes a large purchase on credit without considering the interest rates or a business that rushes to launch a product without proper market research. These instances perfectly illustrate how impatience can compromise our *financial stability*. Quick rewards may seem tempting, but they don't compare to the steady growth from planning.

A WORLD IN A HURRY – *A New Normal*

In both *mental health* and *economics*, impatience causes more harm than good. However, if we step back, slow things down, and think long-term, we can break free from this cycle and lead more *balanced*, fulfilling lives. There is hope for change.

4. The Neuroscience of Impatience

Impatience isn't just a result of external pressures—it's also deeply rooted in how our brains work. Constant exposure to fast-paced, instant stimuli can *rewire* our brain chemistry, affecting how we think, make decisions, and process information. Let's take a closer look at the science behind it.

Brain Rewiring

Today's world is constantly bombarded with *instant gratification*—from checking notifications to quickly scrolling through social media. These activities provide what we call 'instant rewards,' which are quick, pleasurable experiences that trigger the release of dopamine in our brains. This constant stream of *fast-paced stimuli* can have a tangible impact on how our brains operate. Our brains start to rewire, with chemicals like *dopamine* being triggered more frequently, especially when we get those quick rewards. Over time, this leads to a decrease in our ability to focus and an increase in *impulsivity*.

Example: Decreased Attention Span

Think about how we've become accustomed to *short-form content* (TikTok, Instagram Stories, etc.). These platforms are designed to grab our attention for a few seconds at a time. Our brains become accustomed to this quick reward cycle, making it harder to focus on tasks that require sustained attention. The brain's *dopamine system* craves more frequent rewards; when it doesn't get them, we feel bored or restless. This rewiring makes it challenging to stay focused on one thing for long periods, affecting both our productivity and emotional well-being.

Decision-Making

Impatience doesn't just affect our attention span—it also significantly impacts our decision-making. The desire for instant results often drives us to prioritise *short-term rewards* over long-term benefits. The part of our brain responsible for *impulse control* weakens when constantly exposed to impatience, making us more likely to act on a whim.

Example: Impulsive Choices

Consider the example of someone who buys something on impulse. Let's say they see an ad for a new gadget and feel the urge to buy it immediately. That's *impulsivity* at play. Other impulsive choices could include eating unhealthy food while on a diet or skipping a workout when trying to be more active. The *prefrontal cortex*, which helps us weigh long-term consequences, takes a back seat to the desire for instant satisfaction. This leads to a decision that feels good but may not be beneficial in the long run, whether it's a bad financial decision or an unhealthy habit. When we act on impulses, we make decisions based on instant dopamine rewards, often overlooking the long-term consequences.

In both *brain rewiring* and *decision-making*, impatience makes us more reactive and less thoughtful. However, understanding how it affects us on a *neuroscientific* level can empower us to take steps toward retraining our brains to be more patient and deliberate in our choices. The challenge is to break the cycle of instant rewards and retrain ourselves to embrace slower, more thoughtful processes.

Manifestations Of Patience

The rise of *one-click purchases*, *same-day deliveries*, and *streaming platforms* where we can skip all the waiting time has completely changed the game. These innovations make life a lot easier, but have lowered our patience. A few seconds of waiting can now feel like forever, and that impatience starts spilling into all areas of life. We're quick to pick up our phones in the middle of conversations, and when our emotional needs aren't met instantly, it can strain relationships.

Impatience isn't just an occasional feeling anymore—it's become a part of how we live, work, and interact with others. Today, we're constantly rushing to get things done, chase after quick results, and stay connected, all driven by impatience.

On a bigger scale, impatience also affects how we make decisions and approach progress. Take *political discourse*—it's often reduced to *soundbites* and *quick reactions*, with no room for proper discussions or thoughtful debate. Policies are frequently rushed through to appease the public in the short term, but this usually means sacrificing more informed, long-term solutions. It's a similar story with the *environment*: impulsive decisions over the decades have led to crises that require urgent, thoughtful action.

Impatience doesn't just affect our digital lives. There is constant pressure at work to meet deadlines and deliver results quickly. We skip proper planning or thoughtful decision-making because we want to finish soon. This rush to complete everything in record time can lead to cutting corners, focusing solely on quick wins, and sacrificing the broader perspective. The result? *Burnout, poor outcomes*, and the feeling of constantly being overwhelmed by the pressure to do more in less time.

And, of course, there's the impact on our *mental health*. *Stress*, *anxiety*, and *impulsiveness* are what happen when we expect everything to happen instantly and don't manage our expectations appropriately. When things don't happen as fast as we want, we get frustrated, making it even harder to stay calm and make *well-thought-out decisions*. The more impatient we become, the more *stress* we accumulate, and it becomes increasingly complex to slow down and regain control. It's a vicious cycle, and breaking free isn't easy.

STARVED WORLD – *THE PRICE OF PLAYING WITH PATIENCE*

Impatience has become a regular part of life in a world where we are constantly in a rush. Think about it – when we wait for food, we're already impatient even before it arrives, and when it does, we barely enjoy it because we rushed through it. This is the price we pay for chasing *instant gratification* all the time. We're constantly hurrying to get things done quickly, but that short-term satisfaction often leaves us empty.

Patience, on the other hand, brings true *fulfilment*. It's about taking time to enjoy the process, whether at work, in relationships, or in personal growth.

Regarding *business*, impatience can lead companies to make hasty decisions that may not always yield favorable results in the long run. Look at *Myspace*, for instance—it rushed its expansion without a long-term plan, and now it's just a memory. However, under Steve Jobs, companies like Apple demonstrated that a patient, long-term strategy can lead to lasting success.

Similarly, the rush for quick profits, as seen during the 2008 recession, led to massive economic instability. On the other hand, countries like Singapore have taken the time to invest in education and infrastructure, reaping long-term prosperity.

Impatience can be deadly in *war* and *exploration*. Napoleon's hasty invasion of Russia cost him dearly, whereas General Washington's patient approach during the American Revolutionary War ultimately helped him achieve victory. Similarly, *Roald Amundsen's* slow, methodical journey to the South Pole was more successful than Scott's rushed attempt. It's clear: whether in business, war, or exploration, *patience* often leads to better results.

Even in the *environment*, impatience has led us to unsustainable practices, rushing through resource exploitation without considering the future consequences. We need patience and long-term planning to effectively tackle climate change, rather than relying on quick fixes. Likewise, our culture's impatience for quick results can erode traditions and deeper values. However, when we cultivate patience, we foster lasting change in the environment, culture, or society.

So, while impatience might get us results *faster*, it's often at the cost of *quality, stability,* and deeper *fulfilment*. In a world that's always in a rush, *patience* is the key to lasting success, personal growth, and genuine connection. We don't just get more when we slow down; we get better.

8.
ACCEPT WHAT WE CAN'T CONTROL – *A Reflection*

"Patience is a virtue, but it's also a skill that can be developed." - Dalai Lama.

I've been there—getting frustrated over a delayed flight, cursing the power cut, thinking my impatience might somehow change the situation. But it doesn't. The world keeps moving forward, and impatience leaves me feeling drained. During the 2020 lockdowns, we all faced something uncontrollable that hit us hard. We were stuck, with the world moving slowly, yet there was a strange lesson to be learned.
It was as if the universe was saying, "Take a breath; things can move, just slower." Some people embraced it, using the time to learn new skills, while others raged against the restrictions. The funny thing is that after things started opening up again, we all fell back into the same patterns, forgetting the lessons we learned. The patience we'd adopted vanished once life got back to normal.

It's all about *accepting* what we can't control. Letting go isn't surrendering; it's finding *patience*. It's the strength to focus on the things in our hands while peacefully accepting the rest. That's the thing about *impatience*—it fights the unfixable. However, when we attempt to control what we can't, we often end up feeling exhausted and emotionally drained. We're so focused on pushing against the things we can't change that we miss the opportunities right before us. *On* the other hand, patience teaches us to step back, breathe, and find peace in what is.

We only make ourselves miserable when we resist life's uncontrollable factors, like traffic, weather, or people's actions. I've had my moments—like staring at rainclouds as if my scowl could make them disappear. The thing is, that's a waste of *energy. Epictetus* put it perfectly: "You have power over your mind, not outside events." When we *accept* what we can't control, we free ourselves from the cycle of frustration. *Viktor Frankl*, who survived the horrors of a concentration camp, also understood this. He said, "When we can no longer change a situation, we are challenged to change ourselves." Sometimes, it's not about fixing what's broken but shifting how we respond.

This is where the magic of *patience* happens. It's not about doing nothing but knowing when to act and let go. It's about choosing to respond with *calm* instead of *frustration*. So, the next time something uncontrollable happens, ask yourself: What's the *patient's* response? What can I control here? Maybe that's the real power—finding peace not in controlling everything but in accepting what we can't.

Macro Patience and Micro Controls

As someone with a background in economics, I can draw parallels to *macroeconomics* and *microeconomics*, where *macroeconomics refers to broader, larger-scale trends, and microeconomics deals* with individual, day-to-day actions. I intend to apply these concepts in the context of

Accept What We Can't Control – *A Reflection*

"Accepting What We Can't Control" and cultivate patience to achieve long-term success and personal growth. The same idea applies here: *macro patience* means having patience for long-term goals and understanding that things won't always go as quickly as we'd like. It's about staying committed to the bigger vision and not losing faith when things don't happen immediately.

A notable example of this is Domino's Pizza's turnaround in the 2000s. The company was struggling at the time, and many people doubted its future. Instead of throwing in the towel, Domino's focused on what mattered — their core product: pizza. They streamlined their menu, updated their recipes, and embraced technology to offer better service. Their patience with their larger vision paid off over time, and eventually, Domino's became a global leader in pizza delivery. Sure, they had innovative management strategies, but their *macro patience* — sticking with the plan and enduring the rough patches — made it happen.

Micro *control* focuses on the small, day-to-day actions that help you reach those bigger goals. It's about taking charge of your daily habits, decisions, and efforts, knowing that these small actions, when done consistently, add up to something big. The key here is balance — you need the *macro patience* for the larger vision, but you also need the discipline to stay focused on the minor details that bring that vision to life.

Think of a local startup that grew into something much bigger, like *BrewDog*, a small craft beer company that started in Scotland. BrewDog didn't just rely on the long-term idea of changing the beer industry; they focused heavily on their day-to-day operations — brewing quality beer, marketing it creatively, and building a strong community of customers. Over time, these smaller, focused actions helped them expand and eventually become one of the world's most well-known craft beer brands.

I Lack Patience

It wasn't just the big dream of revolutionising the beer industry, but the small, consistent steps that built the foundation for that dream.

This idea of balancing *macro patience* with *micro control* can also be linked to the thoughts of *Immanuel Kant*, who believed that patience isn't just about waiting — it's about taking steady, rational actions over time. Kant's idea of *practical reason* encourages us to remain patient with long-term goals, but not to ignore the smaller steps we must take to achieve them. In other words, we must continue working on day-to-day tasks while maintaining focus on the bigger picture. When you combine *macro patience* and *micro control*, you don't just survive the ups and downs — you find the rhythm to keep moving forward, no matter what challenges come your way.

So, when we combine these two, *macro patience* and *micro control* create a strong foundation for success. *Macro patience* allows us to stay on track when things get tough, while micro control helps us focus on what we can do right now to make progress. By embracing both, we can make steady progress toward our goals, one small but intentional step at a time.

Navigating Fixed Structures

Aren't most of us caught in a system that feels like it's built to frustrate us? Whether it's endless paperwork for a visa, mind-boggling tax rules, or outdated corporate policies, we all encounter these *rigid structures* that seem to have no flexibility. It's like trying to turn a ship with a paddle—no matter how much effort you put in, it doesn't budge. *My impatience* always kicks in when I'm faced with these systems. It's like yelling at a brick wall, hoping it will give way.

Accept What We Can't Control – *A Reflection*

Take the example of European farmers in 2023, who went to great lengths to block roads in protest of EU trade delays that harmed their profits. They had every reason to be frustrated—bills don't wait. But despite their loud protests, nothing changed. That's what impatience feels like: intense, loud, but often just banging your head against something immovable.

However, patience isn't just sitting back and doing nothing—*it's about being clever and working with the system, not against it.* The global effort to ban single-use plastics began in 2015. Activists didn't just storm parliaments or demand instant laws. Instead, they focused on the long game—years of lobbying, collecting data, and gently nudging governments in the right direction.

By 2015, their persistent efforts had led to 50 countries banning single-use plastics, making a significant dent in ocean waste. It wasn't a quick fix, but strategic patience—playing the long game with a clear plan. That kind of patience works, not by forcing a change but by slowly pushing against the system in a way it can't ignore.

When dealing with a system built to last, you've got to realise it won't move quickly, if at all. *Systems, such as government policies, corporate hierarchies, or global markets, are designed for stability.* They're not made to pivot every time something goes wrong. This is where impatience often hits a brick wall.

In 2018, *gig* workers in the UK went on *strike* over delivery apps that set brutal pay rates without room for negotiation. They protested, tweeted, and railed against the system, but the pay algorithms barely budged. Why? Because the system is slow, with layers of decision-makers and established structures that can't be changed overnight.

I Lack Patience

Dumb things that we wish to throw at someone while sitting in a queue at the tax office, feeling my impatience boil over as the clerk shrugs and says, *"It's the process."* It's frustrating, but fighting the system head-on is like shouting at a mountain to move. It's not going anywhere, and you're just exhausting yourself.

This is where patience comes in, but not the kind that involves sitting back and hoping things will change on their own. *Patience* means taking small, manageable steps, even in an unyielding system.

As *Lao Tzu* wisely said, *"A journey of a thousand miles begins with a single step."* Patience in this context is about realising that you can't change the entire system overnight, but you can take that first step. You don't have to win the war all at once. The trick is to work within the system's boundaries and take control of what you can, making gradual progress even when the structure doesn't move.

So, while it's easy to get frustrated and try to force change, real success comes from understanding that systems are built to last, not to shift at your command.

Patience isn't about giving up—it's about playing the long game, finding ways to work within the rules, and slowly making the changes you want to see, one step at a time. This approach empowers you, giving you control and reducing stress.

EMBRACING LIFE'S UNCERTAINTY

Countless factors influence our patience. In the *Continuum Framework*, we analysed how patience and impatience can coexist within us and how it often takes a situation to alter that balance. These shifts can stem from internal and external sources, ultimately defining our actions. But more often than not, external factors trigger impatience. Impatience erupts when we battle things beyond our control—weather, delays, chance. I've cursed a late bus as if shouting at it would make it go faster.

In 2021, the *COVID-19 pandemic-induced supply chain crisis* caused ports to be thrown into disarray. Companies were furious, but no amount of yelling made those ships move. The world's unpredictable nature—floods, earthquakes, changing seasons—reminds us that some things can't be controlled. And then there's time, the one thing none of us can hold onto. We stress about deadlines, acting as if worrying will slow down time. *Mortality*, too—thinking about the shortness of life often sparks impatience as we scramble to 'get things done.' *Chance* and the unknowns of life push us to demand answers, like when I've stressed over vague plans, thinking somehow that *stressing* will bring clarity. The more we try to fight the uncontrollable, the more *impatient* we become, yet it never speeds things up. *On* the other hand, patience might help us move forward without losing our cool.

ACTIVE AND INACTIVE PATIENCE

At times, we find it difficult to distinguish between *patience* and *impatience*, and we often subconsciously live with this distinction in our daily lives, unaware of the underlying mode in which we are operating. We may not always recognise when engaging in *active patience* versus *inactive patience*, as it can feel like flipping a switch between the two, depending on how we activate our minds and thoughts.

Let's understand this with an example—when stuck in traffic, one might experience two very different forms of patience. In *active patience*, the driver might use the time to listen to a podcast, plan their day, or practice deep breathing, thereby transforming the waiting period into an opportunity for *self-improvement* and *reflection*.

This approach aligns with *Viktor Frankl's* concept of *meaning-making*, where, even under challenging circumstances, we have the power to find purpose. *Active patience* involves engaging our thoughts in ways that contribute positively to our well-being rather than letting frustration take over.

In contrast, *inactive patience* might involve simply sitting and waiting passively, hoping for the traffic to clear, without actively managing the feelings of *impatience*. This form of patience mirrors the concept of *learned helplessness*, as described by *Martin Seligman*, where an individual repeatedly faced with uncontrollable situations may stop trying to influence the outcome, accepting the wait without attempting to make the experience meaningful.

Inactive patience often leads to a passive endurance of the situation, leaving us feeling helpless or resigned.

Active patience fosters *growth* and *self-control*, as seen in *Carol Dweck's* concept of a *growth mindset*, where challenges are viewed as opportunities for development. We engage with the moment with active patience, allowing us to grow through the experience.

However, *inactive patience* can lead to *frustration* and stagnation as one surrenders to the situation without engaging in any productive action. By choosing *active patience*, we transform waiting into a space for *growth* and purpose, whereas *inactive patience* often leaves us stuck and fixated on the uncontrollable aspects of the situation.

Key Differences:

√ **Engagement vs. Endurance**: *Active patience* requires engagement, whereas inactive patience involves enduring and accepting the situation.

√ **Purposeful Action vs. Resignation**: *Active patience* might involve making productive use of time, whereas *inactive patience* could lead to a sense of resignation without proactive efforts to ease the wait.

Active *patience* is often more empowering and beneficial because it combines patience with purpose, allowing us to use the time effectively. Inactive *patience* may involve waiting without much personal growth or engagement. By choosing *active patience*, we shift our focus from endurance to actively developing ourselves.

SOCIAL DYNAMICS: *ACCEPTING OTHERS' CHOICES*

We can't control the *actions*, *pace*, or *decisions* of others. It's easy to get *impatient* when someone isn't moving at the desired speed, especially when their actions impact us. Whether it's a colleague working slowly on a project or a friend making choices we disagree with, impatience can easily take hold. However, if we allow that impatience to fester, it often damages relationships.

A 2022 study by *Harvard Business Review* found that remote work challenges led to a 20% increase in conflicts, often due to unrealistic *expectations*. This demonstrates how impatience can negatively influence our interactions.

On the other hand, *patience* is about accepting that others have their own pace. Instead of pressuring them, we can support them through *active listening*, which helps to rebuild *trust*. For instance, a manager who listens rather than imposes urgency creates stronger relationships (Forbes, 2023).

Philosopher *Simone Weil* referred to *attention* as "pure generosity," suggesting that when we offer others our full focus, we value their *thoughts* and *feelings as a genuine expression of care*. This type of attentiveness fosters *understanding* and can mend strained relationships, fostering a sense of empathy and connection.

When the actions of others—whether friends, family, or colleagues—trigger impatience, it's vital to step back and give them space. Rather than reacting immediately, we can ask ourselves: *How can patience help resolve this situation?* Practising patience isn't about tolerating flaws; it's about encouraging *growth*, fostering *understanding*, and creating room for *collaboration*. This approach fosters a sense of respect and consideration for others.

Why We Try to Control Others

It's natural to want things to go our way. Impatience often creeps in when someone is late, disagrees with us, or doesn't meet our expectations. We may find ourselves thinking, *"Make them hurry up! Make them agree!"* It feels empowering when others act in ways we expect, reinforcing our sense of *control*. I've been guilty of this, as when I kept pestering a friend to join a group chat without considering that they were already overwhelmed.

That pressure only pushed them away. Why do we do this? It's because we believe we can shape others' actions—how fast they work, what they say, how they behave. However, the truth is, we cannot. People have their minds, schedules, and struggles. Trying to control them is like trying to

ACCEPT WHAT WE CAN'T CONTROL – *A Reflection*

make the *wind* blow your way—a futile effort that leads to stress and strains relationships.

During the 2020 lockdown, many families found themselves cooped up together, and impatience surged. Parents snapped at kids over slow homework, and siblings argued over screen time—*tensions* in UK homes increased by 30% (BBC, 2020). Everyone wanted others to act in ways that would make life easier, but pushing didn't help. It only created frustration. *However, patience involves accepting that others have* ways of doing things. It's not about agreeing with them, but about allowing them to be, even when difficult.

For example, during the lockdown, a teacher in Manchester accepted her students' challenges—slow *Wi-Fi*, crowded homes—and offered *flexible deadlines*. Rather than scolding, she checked in with her students to provide them with support.

By the end of the term, her class was engaged, and her grades improved (TES, 2020). Her patience and willingness to let students move at their own pace helped build *trust* and reduce *stress*.

Case Study:
Apple and Epic Games Lawsuit - Accepting Others' Choices

The legal dispute between Apple and Epic Games, a leading game developer, is a key example of how accepting others' choices and adopting a balanced approach can help manage conflict, especially under public scrutiny. Epic challenged Apple's App Store policies, which include a 30% commission on in-app purchases and strict distribution guidelines, criticising them as monopolistic and harmful to consumer choice. This triggered a high-profile legal battle, with divided public opinion—some supported Epic's call for openness, while others backed Apple's control over its ecosystem.

Rather than responding with hostility, Apple chose a measured response. It acknowledged the differing needs of consumers and developers, choosing not to impose its views. By recognising various perspectives, Apple avoided further polarisation and actively encouraged dialogue as a key tool in conflict management.

This approach enabled Apple to manage the controversy without alienating its users. Apple showed empathy and patience by engaging in open discussions with developers and consumers, reframing the issue as a balance—finding middle ground between business interests and user needs. As a result, Apple preserved its brand image while upholding its business model.

This case underscores the value of respecting differing opinions. It illustrates how a considerate, inclusive stance can lead to constructive outcomes, foster understanding, and help maintain positive relationships. Accepting others' choices is often a wise and practical path through complex challenges in both business and personal settings.

9.
LEADERSHIP IN AN IMPATIENT WORLD

"Patience is a virtue, and I'm learning it slowly." - Bill Murray.

I once came across an encouraging statement: *"Leaders who emerge from hardship often make the most significant impact in an impatient world."* I wholeheartedly agree, as their experiences shape them, teaching them how to handle situations, overcome challenges, and, most importantly, maintain a calm and mature approach—qualities often linked to patience.

While many leaders are impulsive or act out of impatience, their actions are usually dictated by the demands of the situation. A leader who knows how to strike the right balance between *patience* and *impatience*, understanding when to act swiftly and when to wait, is the kind of leader who truly excels. They wield *patience* and *impulsiveness* as tools, knowing when to apply each with precision without letting either dominate their decision-making process. This balance is not a sign of weakness, but a strength that ensures effective leadership.

I Lack Patience

Leaders from the past and present have always faced immense pressure to deliver quick results, driven by the demand for *instant gratification*, *rapid innovation*, and *immediate outcomes*. While the challenges and context may vary, these expectations can still feel overwhelming. However, effective leadership requires a balance of *adaptability*, *empathy*, *strategic foresight*, and a focus on creating a *sustainable impact*. Patience plays a crucial role in this, allowing leaders to manage the tension between urgency and long-term vision, and inspiring others to do the same.

Leadership is not just about responding to immediate demands, but also about creating an environment that nurtures sustainable growth and positive change. Leaders who instill patience within their teams, while maintaining agility and resilience, contribute significantly to the world around them. As Simon Sinek wisely said, "The role of a leader is not to come up with all the great ideas.

The role of a leader is to create an environment in which great ideas can happen." This statement highlights the crucial role of leaders in creating an environment that enables others to thrive, making them feel empowered and valued.

However, a leader's impatience can have a detrimental impact on team dynamics. Research has shown that 71% of employees report that their leaders' impatience impacts their *productivity* and *job satisfaction* (Harvard Business Review). Consider Satya Nadella of Microsoft, who successfully grew the company through a *patient, strategic approach*. His focus on collaboration and thoughtful decision-making has led to substantial long-term growth.

On the other hand, we have Elon Musk, whose *impulsivity* was on full display when he took over X (formerly Twitter). While Musk's bold moves may have transformed the business in some way, the turmoil and aggression surrounding his leadership style are a stark reminder of the potential risks associated with an *impulsive* approach. His leadership showcases how acting with impatience can lead to upheaval, affecting not only the organisation's stability but also its reputation.

In a world that demands quick fixes and constant innovation, a great leader knows that the right balance between *patience* and *impulsivity* is crucial to achieving success without compromising the well-being of their team or the company's long-term vision. This balance not only enables leaders to be genuinely effective in navigating the challenges of an impatient world but also empowers them to make decisions with confidence. However, it's also important to note that being too patient can lead to missed opportunities and a lack of agility, both of which are crucial in leadership.

The Power of Patience – *A Leadership Imperative*

Patience is often seen as a *virtue*, but it is much more than that for leaders. It is about *practising patience* at every step—each decision, each thought process, and every challenge that comes your way. As a leader, you are constantly expected to make decisions that can either make or break the situation, and those decisions must be made with calmness and *composure*. It is not just about understanding why patient leaders tend to succeed but about how *patience* can transform your leadership style, evolving how you approach problems and shaping your decision-making over time.

Patient leaders approach challenges rationally, making thoughtful choices that solve problems and create opportunities for growth and

I LACK PATIENCE

improvement. While experience plays a significant role, leaders at any level must remain patient, engage in open discussions, listen to diverse perspectives, and be receptive to feedback. This approach not only enables you to navigate complex situations while maintaining your values, but also underscores the importance of patience in leadership.

One of the real benefits of being a patient leader is how it helps avoid the *short-term pitfalls* that can come from acting too quickly. Impulsive decisions may give you quick results, but they often lead to setbacks for you and your team. On the other hand, patient leaders take their time to *assess risks*, consider the long-term *consequences*, and make choices that align with their broader vision. This allows them to address immediate challenges and set a path for *sustainable success*.

Take Jeff Bezos, for example. Instead of focusing on short-term profits, Bezos took a patient, long-term approach by reinvesting Amazon's earnings into *infrastructure* and *innovation*. While many leaders might have rushed to cash in on immediate returns, Bezos was thinking about the future. Moreover, look where that patience got him—Amazon is now a *global powerhouse*, completely changing the retail game. His ability to focus on *sustainable growth* rather than short-term gains demonstrates the decisive impact of patient leadership.

Leaders prioritising a *long-term vision* understand that *stability* and *innovation* are not mutually exclusive. The constant pressure of instant gratification does not sway them; instead, they work patiently to build a strong foundation for future growth. This kind of leadership fosters an environment where *creativity* can flourish, and *strategic initiatives* can take root, leading to success that is not fleeting but truly enduring. By keeping your eyes on the *bigger picture*, you're setting yourself up for success and building *trust* and *resilience* within your team, empowering them to tackle new challenges and achieve long-lasting growth. This approach instills a sense of optimism and forward-thinking in leaders and their teams.

Moreover, when a crisis strikes, that is when patience proves itself to be a strategic advantage. Leaders who act impulsively often make reactionary decisions that exacerbate the situation. But patient leaders? They take a moment to step back, assess the situation, consider the broader implications, and make well-thought-out, strategic responses. This way, they handle the crisis effectively, without creating more disruption than necessary, which gives them a sense of control and preparedness. Patience helps leaders steer their organisations through uncertainty, ensuring they stay on track even in the most challenging times.

How Most Leaders Thrive In an Impatient World

In the modern landscape, we are all exposed to *instant access* to information, *real-time feedback*, and *on-demand solutions*—it is everywhere. Have you ever noticed how we expect everything to happen instantly? Everything is just a click away, from sending a quick email to checking a product review online. It's not just in our personal lives—this rush and pressure have also crept into the workplace. Employees, customers, and investors expect *prompt responses and tangible results*. But let us be real, it's not easy to keep up, right?

Consider this: ***fleeting attention spans,*** where people crave *concise, impactful* communication, *compressed timelines* that push projects to tight deadlines, and *elevated expectations*—all of this while markets constantly change, demanding *innovation* and *adaptation* at every turn. No pressure

I Lack Patience

at all, right? But how can leaders thrive in such a chaotic environment? They need to find that sweet spot between responsiveness and resilience to excel. And the secret? It's about striking a balance between speed and careful thought, adopting a solid approach.

Let's talk about **agile *communication***. Leaders must ensure their teams and stakeholders are always in the loop when impatience runs high. How can that be done? First, keep updates *clear*, *timely*, and *transparent*. Think of companies like Apple—quick, sharp messaging that does not overwhelm, yet keeps everyone on the same page. And what about social media? Companies use it to gather *real-time feedback*, addressing concerns before they spiral. Have you ever seen a company turn negative feedback into something positive in real-time? That is agile communication in action.

Now, **speed is *crucial***—but do not fall into the trap of rushing decisions. Who's been there before? Making a snap decision only to have it backfire later on? It's tough. Leaders who succeed don't just *react*—they *strategise*. How? By *harnessing data* to guide their decisions, they empower their teams to act quickly while maintaining *oversight*. Think of Amazon—they use *real-time insights* to make quick and strategic decisions. It's not just about speed; it's about making wise choices.

Speaking of teams, let's talk about **building *resilient* and *innovative* teams**. We were all under pressure to deliver *yesterday*, but constant pressure can wear people out, right? So, how do great leaders keep their teams *energised* and *creative*? By fostering a space where failure is not feared but seen as part of the process. Google is famous for its *20% time*, which allows employees to work on passion projects. How cool is that? Leaders create an environment where creativity thrives by *investing* in skills and giving teams the tools to adapt. The result? Teams stay agile, delivering *quick wins* while staying aligned with the big picture.

Now, let's dig into **leading with *empathy***. When impatience takes over, frustration builds quickly, right? As a leader, *understanding* the pressures your team is facing makes all the difference. Leaders who show *empathy* don't just manage—they support. Think of Microsoft—leaders there show how *empathy* in the workplace can boost *morale*, even when things get tough. Supporting your team goes beyond just giving them tasks; it's about creating a space where they feel valued and heard.

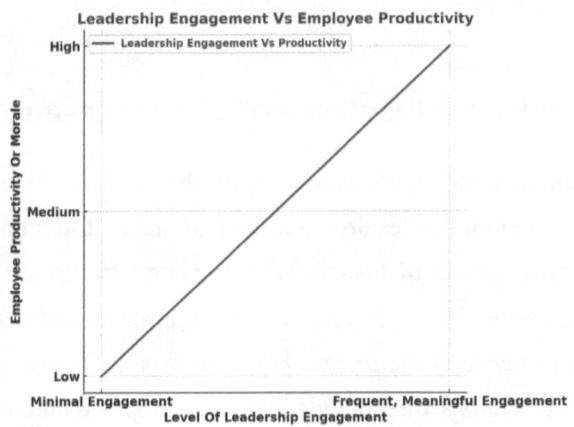

Finally, what about **anchoring in *purpose*?** When the clock is ticking and everyone's racing for results, how do leaders focus on what matters? It is easy to get swept up in the rush, but *purpose* is the compass that keeps you grounded. Leaders who align their actions with their organisation's *values* can inspire their teams, even during stressful times. Take Elon Musk—despite all the pressure, his goal of creating a *sustainable future* with *Tesla* and *SpaceX* keeps him and his teams moving forward. It's about sticking to your purpose, even when the world demands results *yesterday*.

To sum up, thriving as a leader in today's impatient world is about striking a balance between speed and thoughtfulness, empathy and *strategic foresight*, and achieving both *short-term wins* and *long-term success*. Effective leaders communicate effectively, empower their teams, foster resilience, and stay grounded in their purpose while inspiring their teams to work toward a shared goal.

How will you lead in an impatient world? The choice is yours.

APPLYING "EXPECTANCY THEORY" IN LEADERSHIP

In an *impatient* world, particularly within the workplace, leaders often struggle to achieve quick results while maintaining long-term productivity. As impatience grows in fast-paced environments, understanding its underlying causes becomes crucial. One approach that stands out in tackling *impatience* is *Victor Vroom's Expectancy Theory*. This theory posits that individuals are motivated by the anticipated outcomes of their actions, and impatience can often arise when those outcomes feel delayed or unclear.

Expectancy Theory can provide valuable insights into the nature of impatience at its core, especially in a workplace context. The theory suggests that employees' motivation depends on three primary factors: *expectancy*, *instrumentality*, and *valence*. When applied thoughtfully, these elements can help leaders manage *impatience* and create a more engaged and productive workforce.

1. **Expectancy (Effort → Performance)**: This component refers to the belief that one's effort will result in a specific level of performance. Leaders must ensure employees have the right *resources*, *skills*, and *support* to feel confident that their efforts will achieve the desired outcomes. This is particularly important in reducing *impatience*, as employees are less likely to feel frustrated when they believe their efforts are directly linked to success.

2. **Instrumentality (Performance → Outcome)**: This element emphasizes the perception that performing well will lead to the desired reward. To manage *impatience*, leaders must establish *clear pathways* that acknowledge and reward achievements fairly and consistently. Employees who see a clear connection between their performance and outcomes are less likely to become impatient, as they feel the reward is within reach.

3. **Valence (Value of the Outcome)**: An individual's value on the reward plays a critical role in motivation. Leaders must ensure that rewards align with employees' intrinsic *motivations* and personal *goals*. In an impatient world, where people expect fast results, aligning incentives with what truly matters to individuals can help maintain their drive and focus.

Applying *Expectancy Theory* to the workplace, leaders can also manage impatience more effectively through the following strategies:

☐ **Breaking down big goals into smaller ones**: Large projects can often seem overwhelming, which breeds impatience. However, by dividing them into smaller, manageable tasks, you make the goals more achievable and give your team a sense of accomplishment and progress, empowering them to tackle the tasks at hand.

☐ **Regular check-ins**: Holding regular meetings to provide feedback, celebrate wins, and adjust expectations can help prevent frustration. They also reassure your team that their efforts are recognised and supported, fostering a sense of security and reducing impatience.

☐ **Recognise and reward effort**: Recognising the outcomes and the effort employees put into their work can increase motivation. This practice not only makes employees feel valued and appreciated but also boosts their morale and reduces the sense of impatience when immediate results are not always achievable.

☐ **Foster a sense of purpose**: Helping team members understand how their work contributes to the broader *organisational goals* reinforces the *value* of their efforts, making the outcomes more meaningful and less prone to impatience.

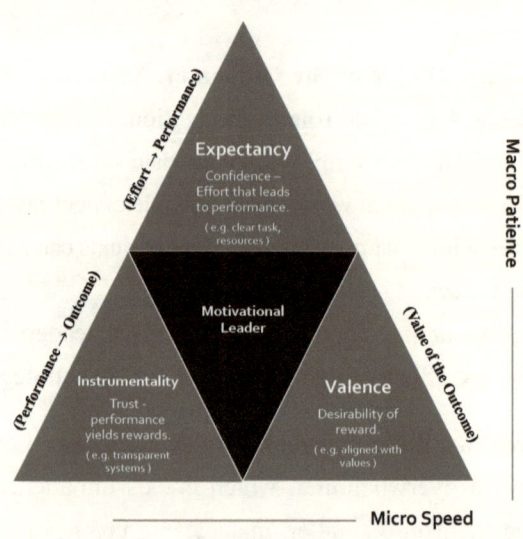

Leaders can effectively address impatience in the workplace by understanding and applying the core components of *Expectancy Theory*— *expectancy*, *instrumentality*, and *valence*. Through clear communication, meaningful rewards, flexibility, and fostering a sense of purpose, leaders can create a motivated, patient, and productive workforce, even in the face of demanding expectations.

Consistently Reliable, Occasionally Extraordinary

In a world that demands instant results, *impatience* has become the norm. Everything feels urgent, and the pressure is on to achieve success quickly. But amidst this rush, there's a type of leader who stands out: the *consistently reliable* one. Think of someone like *Peter Thiel*, co-founder of PayPal. Thiel didn't build PayPal overnight. His leadership wasn't about constant *extraordinary* breakthroughs but about creating something reliable, step by step. This steady progress didn't happen quickly, but it laid a solid foundation for the following exceptional moments—such as PayPal becoming the dominant online payment platform.

Now, compare this with the idea of extraordinary leadership. Leaders like *Richard Branson* have a history of making bold moves and creating spectacular businesses. But even Branson's extraordinary moments wouldn't have had the same impact if they were daily occurrences. *Outstanding* results are rare, and their value is amplified because they are built on consistent, reliable work behind the scenes.

In an impatient world, it's easy to want results *now*, but a *reliable* leader teaches patience. They don't promise quick fixes. Instead, they create a *steady rhythm* of progress, where the team knows that although results may take time, they are inevitable with consistent effort. Like Warren Buffett, a reliable leader does not rush for quick wins. He's built his fortune by focusing on long-term, reliable growth, waiting patiently

I Lack Patience

for the right opportunities. He said, "The stock market is a device for transferring money from the impatient to the patient."

The key here is *balance*. A reliable leader is *patient*; through that patience, they create a culture where extraordinary moments can happen.

On the other hand, *impatience* often leads to burnout and poor decisions. Focusing on instant results is easy, but leaders who chase quick fixes can lose sight of the bigger picture. For instance, a leader impatient for immediate results might push their team too hard, leading to burnout and decreased productivity. A leader who fosters patience within their team helps them stay focused on long-term goals, building the kind of trust that turns ordinary efforts into extraordinary outcomes.

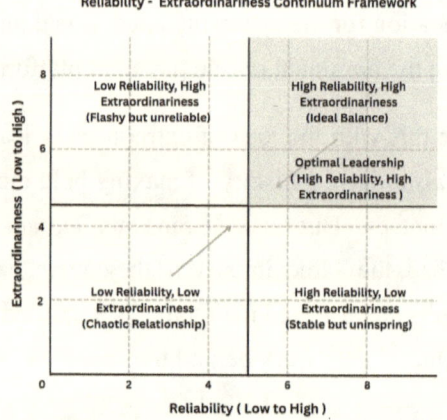

So, how does a leader strike a balance between being *reliable* and *extraordinary*? It's about knowing when to deliver steady, consistent results and when to take a bold step. *Simon Sinek* once said, "Leadership is not about being in charge. It's about taking care of those in your charge." A reliable leader builds trust, ensures steady progress, and delivers an extraordinary moment that makes all the patience worth it when the time is right. I encourage you to reflect on your leadership style and consider incorporating patience into your approach.

In the end, the consistently reliable leader doesn't just manage *impatience*—they transform it into something productive. They show that while *extraordinary* moments are powerful, the real magic happens in the consistent, patient work that leads up to them. For instance, a leader's patience can turn a team's frustration into a problem-solving session, or a customer's impatience into an opportunity to provide exceptional service.

CASE STUDY:
SATYA NADELLA AND MICROSOFT'S TRANSFORMATION

When Satya Nadella took over as CEO of Microsoft in 2014, the company struggled to remain relevant in a rapidly evolving tech landscape. Nadella's leadership focused on long-term goals, particularly transforming Microsoft into a *cloud-first* company, rather than rushing into quick solutions.

One of his key moves was the 2016 acquisition of LinkedIn, a strategic decision that aligned with his vision for integrating cloud computing and artificial intelligence. This wasn't about short-term profits but securing Microsoft's future.

Nadella made swift, impactful decisions, such as embracing mobile by offering *Office 365* on iOS and Android, immediately improving Microsoft's standing in the mobile space.

However, Nadella's leadership demonstrates that managing impatience is about maintaining a long-term vision, making necessary quick decisions, and staying committed to steady, sustainable growth. For instance, when faced with a crisis, a leader can be patient in understanding the situation before making a quick decision on how to address it. Under his guidance, Microsoft became one of the world's most valuable companies, demonstrating that consistent and patient leadership can yield extraordinary results.

10.
CULTIVATING PATIENCE

"With love and patience, nothing is impossible." - Daisaku Ikeda.

You're on a train, excited for the journey ahead, only to find someone's taken your seat. Now, you've got a choice—ask them to move and show your ticket, or sit in one of the available empty seats. That vacant seat is just as good as the one you booked, but here's the thing—your mind starts racing. Inconvenience creeps in, irritation builds up, and maybe even a bit of ego kicks in. "This shouldn't be happening," you think. The attitude takes a toll, and suddenly, you're on the verge of frustration.

So, what do you do? You could make a scene, demand your seat, and get into a back-and-forth, or adjust, sit down, and move on. The journey is short, after all, and you'll be off the train soon enough. The key here is about mindset. It's about accepting that things won't always go as planned, and instead of fighting it, you learn to adapt.

In moments like this, mindfulness plays a considerable role. It's about noticing that the irritation is building up, but instead of letting it take over,

I Lack Patience

you choose to let it go. Mindfulness is a powerful tool that helps you realise the inconvenience isn't life-ending, and the energy spent fighting it might be better used elsewhere. When you focus on what matters—like that you'll reach your destination eventually—you can let go of the small stuff and focus on what's important.

Patience in moments of instant gratification is all about understanding that not everything will unfold the way you expect, but that doesn't mean it's the end of the world. It's about being mindful of your reaction and realising that adjusting your mindset can make all the difference.

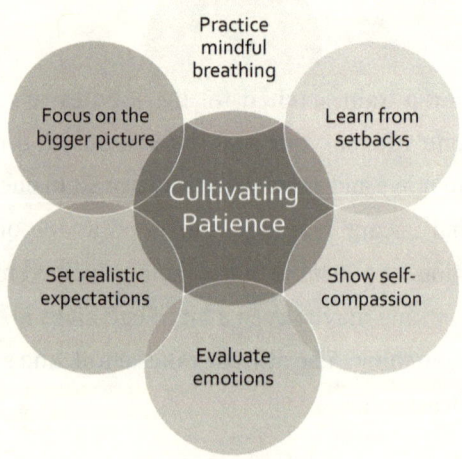

Emotional Intelligence and Self-Awareness –
Structure Patience

Imagine being in a meeting where tensions are high and frustration is rising. You feel the impatience building, yet you *pause*, take a deep breath, and regain control. This is where *emotional intelligence* (EI) and *self-*

Cultivating Patience

awareness play a crucial role. EI is the ability to recognise, understand, and manage emotions, not just your own but also those of others. Some individuals seem to have a natural gift for this—they can sense the mood of a room and stay composed under pressure. However, for others, this can be more challenging. The *good news* is that EI is a skill we can all develop.

Self-awareness is key to EI. It's the ability to understand *your emotions*—knowing what triggers them and how they influence your behaviour. The more you *know yourself*, the easier it becomes to notice moments when impatience is about to surface. And here's where the true power of EI and self-awareness shines: *you can transform impatience into patience*, bringing relief. Self-awareness is not merely a skill; it's a *superpower* you can cultivate.

Consider how *different we all are*. Some people are naturally attuned to their own emotions and those of others, while others may not recognize them until it's too late. This is where developing both emotional intelligence (EI) and self-awareness is beneficial. With EI, you can identify impatience before it overwhelms you, and with self-awareness, you gain the tools to manage it effectively. Whether taking a *breath*, stepping away for a moment, or *shifting perspective*, the key is to be *proactive*, not *reactive*. This proactive approach gives you a sense of control over your emotions and reactions.

Take *Oprah Winfrey*, for example. She's widely known for her remarkable EI. She can read people's emotions and respond with *kindness* and *patience*. Oprah doesn't just react—she's self-aware enough to identify when she's feeling triggered, enabling her to remain calm and composed. This blend of emotional intelligence (EI) and self-awareness is why she handles even the most stressful situations with grace.

I Lack Patience

Let's say you're at work, *stressed* by looming deadlines, and you feel impatience bubbling up. If you're self-aware, you'll catch that feeling of frustration before it takes over, giving you a sense of control. With EI, you can pause, recognise what's causing it, and choose a different response—perhaps by asking for a little extra time or simply taking a *moment to breathe*. Instead of snapping or rushing, you can act patiently, remaining in control and keeping things positive for everyone around you.

By focusing on EI and *self-awareness*, you can begin recognising your emotional triggers, understanding why impatience arises, and managing those emotions before they take control. With practice, responding with patience becomes easier, and you'll find it helps you build stronger relationships and handle life's challenges with greater *calm* and *control*. It's not about *perfection*—it's about progress. Each step you take, no matter how small, brings you closer to a more *patient* and *balanced* version of yourself, motivating you to continue your journey of personal growth.

Meditation and Mindfulness – Reframing Perspective

Patience isn't something we're born with—it's a *skill* we can develop. Like many, I've struggled with it. *Meditation* never came naturally, and my *impatience* often won. Even when I'm *mindful* of my choices, I still react. If this sounds familiar, you're not alone. But I've learned that with perseverance, even the most impatient can master the art of patience.

Let's discuss meditation and mindfulness—two powerful practices that can transform our approach to dealing with *frustration*. They're not just about staying calm—they help us *manage stress*, *delay reactions*, and *build emotional control.* With simple routines, you can begin to develop greater patience and resilience. The power to change is in your hands.

Patience isn't just waiting—it's about *reframing how we respond.* These practices make us more *aware* of what's happening inside us, helping us *pause, breathe,* and react more *deliberately.*

Patience *is a journey,* not *a destination.* If you, like me, find it challenging, that's perfectly okay. Some days will be more difficult than others. But with consistent effort, you'll begin to notice a change. Through the power of breath, awareness, and stillness, you'll reshape your responses and become more patient over time.

Remember, it's okay to start small. The results of your efforts, no matter how modest they may seem at first, are *worth it.* Every step you take towards patience is a step towards a more peaceful and fulfilling life.

TIME MANAGEMENT AND PRIORITISATION

Time management is one of those skills we all know we need, but let's be honest: it's not always easy to master. I get it—sometimes, it feels like there's never enough time in the day, or we're always rushing to meet deadlines. And trust me, you're not alone in feeling that way. I struggle with it, too. I remember a time when I was juggling multiple projects and deadlines, and it felt like I was constantly playing catch-up. While I can prioritise my work and personal life, *time management* is something I'm still working on. External factors also play a role in this, impacting how I manage my time. It's a constant learning process, and I'm pushing myself to improve.

I Lack Patience

If you're like me, here's some comforting news: By embracing a few *time management* strategies, you can alleviate stress, regain control, and—surprisingly—cultivate more *patience*. Mastering your time better helps you feel less overwhelmed and brings a profound sense of relief and control, knowing you can handle the day's demands more confidently and calmly.

Now, let's delve into *prioritisation*. We've all experienced those days when everything feels urgent, and it can seem like you're drowning in tasks. The key is to focus on what truly matters. Instead of getting lost in the endless *to-do* list, *prioritisation* empowers you to concentrate on what's most important, giving you more breathing room and, ultimately, more *patience* for the tasks. It's a strategy that puts you in the driver's seat, enhancing your sense of control and confidence.

Effective Time Management Strategies for Reducing Stress and Increasing Patience –

Good *time management* doesn't just help you get things done—it enables you to stay in control and reduce stress, which is crucial for maintaining *patience*. If you're constantly running behind, it's hard to keep calm. Here are some strategies that can help you manage your time better and ultimately build more *patience*:

- **The 2-Minute Rule**: Complete tasks that take less than two minutes immediately. This simple rule prevents small tasks from piling up and overwhelming you, leaving you with more mental space to focus on bigger, more critical projects.

    Instance: Replying to a quick email or scheduling a meeting? Get it done straight away. This keeps your to-do list manageable and helps

Cultivating Patience

you focus on more significant tasks without feeling impatient about the little things. Knowing you're staying on top of your tasks gives you a sense of accomplishment, boosting your motivation and sense of success.

- **The Pomodoro Technique**: This one's simple and effective. Set a timer for 25 minutes, work with focus, and then take a 5-minute break. This technique helps keep your energy and mind fresh, stopping you from feeling burnt out and *impatient*.

Instance: If you're working on a project, use this technique to break it into manageable chunks. You'll feel more in control and less rushed.

- **Time Blocking**: Instead of switching between tasks throughout the day, try blocking out specific chunks of time for each activity. This helps you avoid distractions and focus on one thing at a time, which not only reduces stress but also helps you stay *patient* as you work on your tasks without feeling rushed.

Instance: Block out specific emails, meetings, or deep work times. By sticking to these blocks, you'll stop multitasking, which often leads to impatience.

I Lack Patience

When you manage your time effectively, you can approach each task with a calm, measured attitude, rather than rushing through everything and becoming frustrated.

Prioritisation Techniques for Focusing on What's Truly Important –

Time is limited, and we all have too much on our plates. That's where *prioritisation* comes in. By focusing on what truly matters and letting go of what doesn't, you'll avoid the stress of trying to do everything at once, which, as we know, only leads to *impatience*. Here are a few techniques to help you *prioritise* better:

- **The Eisenhower Matrix**: This classic method divides tasks into four categories—urgent and important, important but not urgent, urgent but not necessary, and neither urgent nor important. By focusing on what's urgent and essential, you can tackle the high-priority stuff without getting distracted by things that don't matter as much.

    Instance: If you're working on a big presentation, ensure it's your top priority. Don't get sidetracked by emails or social media until the main task is done.

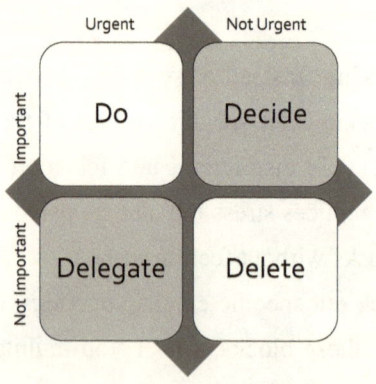

CULTIVATING PATIENCE

- **The ABCDE Method**: Label your tasks from A (most important) to E (least significant). Tackle the A tasks first and leave the E tasks until last. This simple but effective method ensures you focus on the right things at the right time.

Instance: If you have a report due and a minor task like filing paperwork, tackle the report first. The filing can wait.

Categorise tasks and execute them by importance

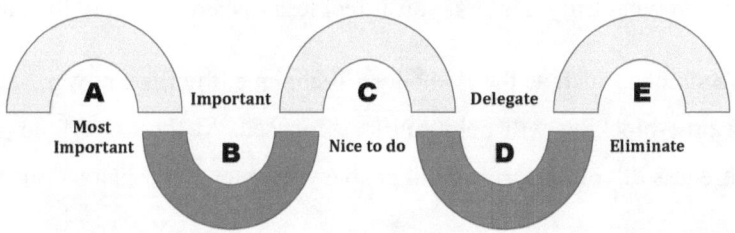

- **The 80/20 Rule (Pareto Principle)** states that 80% of your results come from 20% of your efforts. Identify the 20% of tasks that move the needle and *prioritise* those. By focusing on high-impact tasks, you can maximise your productivity and stop wasting time on less important things.

Instance: Focus on the big wins, like closing a deal or finishing a key project, and save the smaller tasks for later. You'll get more done without burning out or feeling *impatient*.

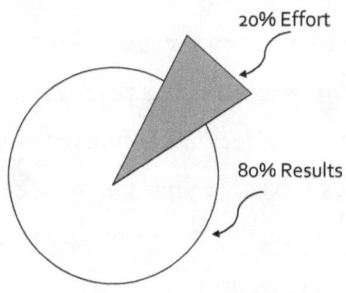

I Lack Patience

When you start prioritising effectively, you'll have more time to focus on what matters. This will reduce your feeling overwhelmed and allow you to approach each task patiently.

Conclusion

Effective *time management* and *prioritisation* are game-changers when managing stress and building *patience*. When you control your time and focus on what truly matters, you'll feel less rushed and more in charge.

Techniques such as the Pomodoro Technique, the Eisenhower Matrix, and time-blocking will help you stay focused. At the same time, self-awareness of your priorities will enable you to let go of distractions.

By mastering these skills, you'll reduce stress and cultivate the *patience* needed to handle life's challenges with a clearer mind and a calm heart.

THE 5-STEP MODEL

To begin training your mind for patience, consider following this simple yet effective 5-step process:

1. **Acknowledge** - Start by **recognising** impatience when it arises. This is not a sign of weakness but a powerful tool for self-awareness. By acknowledging your feelings before reacting, you are in control. By pausing to acknowledge your emotions, you can choose your response instead of reacting out of habit, thereby fostering a sense of self-awareness and control.

Actionable Tip: Pay attention to moments in your day when you feel impatient. Recognise the trigger—whether it's waiting for something, dealing with a challenging person, or facing a delay.

2. Assess - Once you've acknowledged your impatience, it's time to **evaluate** the situation. Ask yourself: How important is this moment? Is it worth the frustration? This helps you gain perspective and separate your emotional reaction from the actual circumstances.

Actionable Tip: Ask yourself, "Does this situation deserve my frustration, or is it something I can simply let go of?" This step requires a moment of pause before moving forward.

3. Adjust - Now, *adjust* your thoughts and actions. Instead of impulsively reacting, choose to adopt a more patient mindset. This shift in thinking can bring a sense of empowerment, as you focus on the bigger picture or reframe the situation as more manageable. This empowerment will make you feel more in control of the problem and less rushed.

Actionable Tip: Reframe your thoughts: "This will pass, and staying calm will help me navigate it more effectively." Adjust your mindset to adopt a longer-term perspective rather than focusing on immediate gratification.

4. Act - With patience in mind, it's time to **take action**. Your actions should reflect calmness and self-control, even in the face of stressful or inconvenient situations.

I Lack Patience

Actionable Tip: Break down your tasks into smaller steps. If you are facing a delay, calmly assess what you can do now rather than worrying about the result. Focus on the process, not just the outcome.

5. Absorb - Finally, *absorb* the lesson. After the moment, reflect on how you handled the situation. What went well? What could you have done better? This reflection is not about self-criticism, but about celebrating your growth and reinforcing your progress in the skill of patience. This celebration will make you feel more positive and less critical.

Actionable Tip: At the end of your day, reflect on the moments where you exhibited patience. Celebrate your successes and identify areas where you can continue to grow.

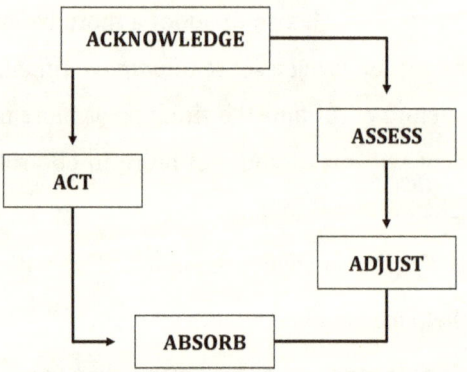

In summary, the 5-step model for cultivating patience involves acknowledging impatience, assessing the situation, adjusting your mindset, acting with patience, and absorbing the lessons learned. This model can help you develop a more patient and controlled approach to life's challenges.

Cultivating Patience

Elon Musk is known for his relentless work ethic, but what stands out is his ability to manage his time effectively. Musk's approach to *time management* is a masterclass in prioritisation and focus. Here's how he makes it work:

- **Time Blocking**: Musk is famous for scheduling his entire day into 5-minute blocks. This method ensures that every moment is accounted for, helping him stay productive and focused without wasting time. By dedicating specific time slots to particular tasks, Musk avoids the usual stress of multitasking.

- **Prioritising What Matters**: Musk's prioritisation ability is key to success. He focuses on the most important aspects, such as product development and engineering, while delegating less critical tasks to others. This way, he avoids getting bogged down in unnecessary details and can stay patient with the big picture.

- **Minimizing Distractions: Musk knows that distractions can consume** valuable time. By keeping his schedule tight and prioritising deep work, he reduces stress and prevents impatience from taking over. His focus on high-priority tasks enables him to make decisions without feeling rushed.

Musk's time management strategy enables him to remain calm and focused, even in the fast-paced tech industry. Applying these principles can help reduce stress and manage your time more effectively, ultimately allowing you to stay more patient throughout your day.

ACTIVITIES

"Patience is a journey, not a destination." Unknown.

Practical Exercises

1. Mindful Breathing

Purpose: To ground yourself in the present moment and reduce impatience.

How to do it:

- ☐ Whenever you feel impatience creeping in, stop what you're doing and take a few deep breaths.
- ☐ Inhale slowly through your nose for a count of four, hold for four seconds, then exhale slowly through your mouth for a count of four.
- ☐ Focus on the sensation of the breath entering and leaving your body.

✓ **Why it works:** This simple breathing exercise helps interrupt the rushing cycle and creates space for a mental reset. It activates the parasympathetic nervous system, helping you to relax and refocus.

2. The 10-Minute Wait Challenge

Purpose: To practice waiting without reacting.

How to do it:

- ☐ Choose a situation in your day where you usually feel impatient, such as waiting in line at the grocery store, being stuck in traffic, or during a long meeting. Allow yourself to wait 10 minutes without looking at your phone, tapping your foot, or fidgeting. Just breathe and observe your thoughts.

I Lack Patience

☐ When 10 minutes are up, reflect on how you felt. Did you experience discomfort? What thoughts ran through your mind?

✓ **Why it works:** This exercise forces you to sit uncomfortably and realise that nothing catastrophic happens when you stop rushing. Over time, you'll build the mental resilience to handle longer waits with more grace.

3. The "Pause and Reflect" Practice

Purpose: The 'Pause and Reflect' Practice is designed to enhance your awareness of impatience triggers and assist you in reframing your reactions.

How to do it:

☐ Stop momentarily the next time you feel impatience rising (perhaps while waiting for something or dealing with an unexpected delay).

☐ Ask yourself: Why am I feeling this way? What can I not control right now? How can I reframe this situation in a positive light?

☐ Take a mental note of the situation and your response. Please write it down later in a journal.

☐ **Why it works:** By consciously pausing and reflecting, you become more aware of the underlying triggers of your impatience. Over time, this self-awareness will help you respond more mindfully instead of reacting impulsively.

4. The "Expectation vs. Reality" Exercise

Purpose: To examine and adjust your expectations to reduce frustration.

ACTIVITIES

How to do it:

- ☐ Choose an area where you tend to get impatient because of unmet expectations (e.g., work deadlines, family schedules, etc.).
- ☐ Please write down your expectations for a situation and then reflect on its reality. How often do things go exactly as you expect? What is a more realistic perspective?
- ☐ After writing down your expectations and reality, note how to adjust your mindset and prepare for challenges.

✓ **Why it works:** This exercise helps you see how our expectations often set us up for impatience. By shifting to more realistic expectations, we can reduce the gap between hope and reality, reducing frustration.

5. Patience in Action: The Slow Task

Purpose: To intentionally practice patience by performing a task slowly and mindfully.

How to do it:

- ☐ Select a simple, routine task—such as folding laundry, washing dishes, or making your bed.
- ☐ Aim to complete this task slowly and be fully aware of each movement. Focus on the details, such as the texture of the fabric, the sound of the water running, or the rhythm of your actions.
- ☐ Resist the urge to rush or multitask. Notice how your body feels as you slow down.
- ☐ Reflect on the experience: How did it feel to perform the task slowly? Did you experience a sense of accomplishment in being fully present and engaged in the task? This exercise can bring a sense of

I LACK PATIENCE

satisfaction and fulfilment that rushing through tasks often does not provide.

✓ **Why it works:** Performing a task mindfully, with full attention and slow deliberation, trains your mind to embrace the process rather than rush to the end. It also helps to integrate patience into your daily routines.

6. The "I Can Control This" Affirmation

Purpose: To reclaim control over situations that trigger impatience.

How to do it:

☐ When you encounter a situation that makes you feel impatient (e.g., waiting for someone, facing a delay), pause and silently repeat the affirmation: "I can control how I respond to this situation."

☐ By acknowledging that you can only control your reaction, you empower yourself to let go of the need to control the external circumstances. This affirmation is a powerful tool that can help you feel more in control and less overwhelmed in situations that trigger impatience.

✓ **Why it works:** This exercise is a quick mental reset that lets you step back from the emotional pull of impatience and regain control over your feelings.

7. Mindful Digital Consumption: Reclaiming Your Time

Purpose: To regain control over your time and reduce the sense of

ACTIVITIES

impatience triggered by excessive screen time. By practising mindful consumption, you can shift your focus from instant gratification to meaningful engagement with your digital environment.

How to do it:

☐ Set specific times for checking emails, social media, and other digital platforms.

☐ During these times, be fully present—avoid distractions and focus only on the task at hand.

☐ When you feel the urge to check your phone or screen outside designated times, pause and ask yourself: "Is this necessary right now?"

☐ Consider using apps or tools that track your screen time to set daily limits.

✓ **Why it works:** Limiting unnecessary digital consumption reduces the constant stimulation that often leads to impatience and distraction. This practice helps you reclaim time, enhance focus, and foster more intentional engagement with the world. Over time, mindful digital consumption creates more space for productive and purposeful actions, reducing the sense of being overwhelmed by constant notifications.

8. Engaging in Physical Activity: Resetting Your Body

Purpose: To reset your body and mind by incorporating regular physical activity, which helps build patience through physical resilience and mental clarity. Exercise encourages the release of endorphins, improving your mood and providing a natural outlet for stress and frustration.

I Lack Patience

How to do it:

- Choose a form of exercise you enjoy, whether walking, running, yoga, or weightlifting.
- Set a regular schedule for physical activity, ideally aiming for at least 30 minutes a day, 3-5 times a week.
- While exercising, focus on your breath, movement, and body sensations. Practice being fully present, rather than thinking about the future or feeling rushed to finish.
- Start with simple exercises and gradually increase the intensity as your fitness improves.

✓ **Why it works:** Physical activity helps to clear the mind and reset your emotional state by reducing stress hormones like cortisol and increasing endorphins. It enhances your overall well-being and allows you to manage impatience better by improving your resilience. By embracing physical activity, you build a stronger body and a more patient mindset.

Conclusion: These practical exercises are small, manageable steps that help build patience over time. They are designed to help you focus and commit to your personal development.

Like any skill, patience takes practice. You can gradually change your default reaction from impatience to calm through self-awareness, mindfulness, and reflection.

The key is to be kind to yourself during this process. Developing patience is not an overnight task, but each small effort brings you closer to mastering the art of patience in an impatient world.

Patience Challenge Quiz – 20 Questions

Instructions:

For each correct answer, give yourself 1 point. Tally up your points at the end of the quiz to determine your score.

Score Range:

- 20/20: Excellent! You have a strong grasp on the concepts of patience and mindfulness, and you're well on your way to mastering the skill of patience.
- 16-19/20: Great work! You have a solid understanding of patience-building concepts and strategies. You're very close to mastering it!
- 11-15/20: Good job! You're making progress, but there are a few areas you could improve on to deepen your understanding of patience.
- 10/20 or below: Keep practicing! Patience is a skill that takes time and effort to develop, so continue applying yourself and practising the exercises.

Question 1:

What does the Impatience Epidemic refer to in modern society?

    A) The widespread lack of patience among individuals.

    B) The daily routine of being patient in various situations.

    C) The acceptance of impatience as a trait.

I Lack Patience

Answer: A - The Impatience Epidemic refers to the widespread lack of patience due to fast-paced living.

Question 2:

Which of the following best defines impatience?

    A) A trait that can't be changed.

    B) A daily impulse or reaction triggered by various factors.

    C) A natural response to situations that don't meet our expectations.

Answer: B - Impatience is a daily impulse, often triggered by external factors, that we can learn to manage.

Question 3:

The Continuum Framework for patience suggests that:

    A) Patience is an all-or-nothing trait.

    B) Patience exists on a spectrum and can vary from person to person.

    C) Patience is a trait that can't be developed.

Answer: B - The Continuum Framework views patience as a spectrum that varies depending on the individual.

Question 4:

Which of the following is a common trigger of impatience?

    A) Receiving immediate results.

    B) Long waits or delays.

ACTIVITIES

C) Practising patience consistently.

Answer: B - Long waits or delays are common triggers of impatience.

Question 5:

What is the psychological impact of chronic impatience?

A) It strengthens personal relationships.

B) It leads to mental stress and emotional burnout.

C) It promotes long-term happiness and peace of mind.

Answer: B - Chronic impatience leads to mental stress and emotional burnout, affecting overall well-being.

Question 6:

What does "shaping patience's path" mean in the context of impatience?

A) Developing techniques to eliminate impatience.

B) Identifying and responding to impatience triggers in a healthy way.

C) Avoiding stressful situations altogether.

Answer: B - Shaping patience's path involves identifying and managing impatience triggers effectively.

Question 7:

Which of the following is a consequence of impatience in relationships?

A) Strengthened communication and understanding.

I Lack Patience

B) Increased connection and mutual respect.

C) Strained communication and misunderstandings.

Answer: C- Impatience can strain relationships.

Question 8:

How does impatience in everyday life affect our overall well-being?

A) It boosts mental clarity and focus.

B) It contributes to increased stress and poor decision-making.

C) It enhances patience in others.

Answer: B - Impatience in daily life leads to stress, poor decision-making, and decreased overall well-being.

Question 9:

Which factor is most likely to fuel impatience in modern society?

A) Slower technological advancements.

B) The fast-paced, instant gratification culture.

C) Increased focus on mindfulness practices.

Answer: B - The fast-paced culture of instant gratification contributes significantly to impatience.

Question 10:

What is the Power of Gradual Shifts in managing impatience?

A) Making drastic changes to reduce impatience.

ACTIVITIES

B) Gradually shifting your mindset and behaviours towards greater patience.

C) Ignoring impatience and pushing through stress.

Answer: B - Involves slowly changing behaviours and mindsets to develop patience.

Question 11:

Which of the following is an effective method for reframing impatience?

A) Suppressing the feeling of impatience until it goes away.

B) Practising mindfulness and questioning the need to rush.

C) Ignoring the situation and walking away.

Answer: B - Involves questioning the urgency and practising mindfulness.

Question 12:

What is the root cause of impatience according to the "Patience Puzzles" model?

A) A lack of understanding of the situation.

B) A desire for instant gratification and control.

C) Complete surrender to circumstances.

Answer: B - Impatience often arises from a desire for immediate results and a lack of control.

Question 13:

Which of the following is considered a social factor that amplifies impatience?

I Lack Patience

   A) Social media fosters comparison and unrealistic expectations.

   B) Engaging in quiet activities that promote reflection.

   C) Building emotional resilience through challenges.

Answer: A - Social media often amplifies impatience by fostering unrealistic expectations and constant comparison.

Question 14:

What is the impact of impatience on personal growth and well-being?

   A) It accelerates growth by pushing us to act faster.

   B) It stunts growth by causing stress and hindering reflection.

   C) It has no impact on personal growth.

Answer: B - Impatience can stunt personal growth by causing stress and preventing thoughtful reflection.

Question 15:

What does "waiting vs. waiting patiently" refer to?

   A) The difference between doing nothing while waiting and actively working during the wait.

   B) The mental state of being calm and focused versus anxious and distracted.

   C) Both A and B.

Answer:C - Waiting patiently involves being calm and focused and using the wait constructively rather than being anxious or distracted.

ACTIVITIES

Question 16:

Which of the following is a growth mindset strategy for overcoming impatience?

    A) Accepting impatience as a permanent part of your personality.

    B) Viewing challenges and delays as opportunities for learning and self-improvement.

    C) Reacting quickly to all situations to avoid waiting.

Answer: B - A growth mindset helps reframe challenges and delays as opportunities to learn and improve.

Question 17:

What is the social pulse about impatience?

    A) A measure of impatience within an individual's social circles.

    B) The growing societal tendency towards impatience in fast-paced environments.

    C) The speed at which society accepts impatience as usual.

Answer: B - The social pulse refers to the growing societal impatience driven by fast-paced living.

Question 18:

What is a common trigger for impatience in the workplace?

    A) Lack of resources or time pressure.

    B) Clear communication and realistic deadlines.

    C) A calm, slow-paced environment.

I Lack Patience

+Answer: A - Time pressure and lack of resources often trigger impatience in the workplace.

Question 19:

What is the scientific basis behind patience and success?

    A) Patience directly correlates with better mental health, which leads to long-term success.

    B) Success depends solely on speed, not patience.

    C) Patience has no scientific effect on success.

Answer: A- Scientific research shows that patience improves mental health and sustained success over time.

Question 20:

Which of the following is a recommended way to develop patience in an impatient world?

    A) Focus on immediate rewards and avoid long-term planning.

    B) Embrace uncertainty, practice mindfulness, and manage expectations.

    C) Always act quickly to maintain control.

Answer:B - Developing patience involves embracing uncertainty, practising mindfulness, and managing expectations.

"You may review your score and pinpoint where you need to ignite the spark that transforms impatience into patience."

FURTHER REFERENCES

FOR READING

Mindfulness and Presence

1. "The Power of Now" by Eckhart Tolle: Living in the present moment.
2. "Wherever You Go, There You Are" by Jon Kabat-Zinn: Mindfulness for inner calm.
3. "The Miracle of Mindfulness" by Thich Nhat Hanh: Practical mindfulness advice.
4. "Mindfulness in Plain English" by Bhante Henepola Gunaratana: Cultivating mindfulness.
5. "Mindfulness for Beginners" by Jon Kabat-Zinn: Introduction to mindfulness.
6. "Be Here Now" by Ram Dass: Mindfulness and being present.
7. "The Untethered Soul" by Michael A. Singer: Letting go of mental barriers.
8. "Radical Acceptance" by Tara Brach: Developing self-compassion through mindfulness.
9. "The Compassionate Mind" by Paul Gilbert: Developing self-compassion.
10. "Presence: Bringing Your Boldest Self to Your Biggest Challenges" by Amy Cuddy: Embracing presence and confidence.

Patience and Personal Growth

1. "The Power of Patience" by M.J. Ryan: Cultivating patience for personal growth.

I Lack Patience

2. "The Art of Waiting": Understanding patience and waiting.

3. "Patience: The Art of Peaceful Living" by Allan Lokos: Cultivating patience.

4. "The Art of Stillness" by Pico Iyer: Reflecting on patience.

5. "Waiting: A Nonviolent Revolution" by David Whyte: Poetic exploration of patience.

6. "The Gifts of Imperfection" by Brené Brown: Embracing imperfection.

7. "Daring Greatly" by Brené Brown: Embracing vulnerability.

8. "Atomic Habits" by James Clear: Building patience through habits.

Emotional Intelligence and Relationships

1. "Emotional Intelligence": Understanding and managing emotions.

2. "The Art of Listening" by Michael P. Nichols: Listening for better relationships.

3. "The 5 Levels of Leadership" by John C. Maxwell: Leadership growth.

4. "Leaders Eat Last" by Simon Sinek: Fostering team trust.

5. "The Leadership Challenge" by James M. Kouzes & Barry Z. Posner: Effective leadership.

Productivity and Success

1. "Deep Work" by Cal Newport: Focus and productivity.

2. "The Dip" by Seth Godin: Balanced approach to patience.

3. "The Obstacle Is the Way" by Ryan Holiday: Overcoming obstacles with patience.

Activities

4. "Mindset: The New Psychology of Success" by Carol Dweck: Transforming life with a growth mindset.

Philosophy and Meaning

1. "The Art of Happiness" by Dalai Lama and Howard Cutler: Patience for a contented life.

2. "Man's Search for Meaning" by Viktor Frankl: Finding meaning and patience in suffering.

3. "The Paradox of Choice" by Barry Schwartz: Limiting choices for well-being.

4. "The Art of Choosing" by Sheena Iyengar: Understanding choice psychology.

These categories help group books by themes, making it easier to find relevant recommendations.

Online Courses

Mindfulness and Well-being

1. "The Science of Well-Being" (Coursera): A Yale University course on happiness, patience, and psychological principles.

2. "Mindfulness for Wellbeing and Peak Performance" (Future Learn): Building resilience and overcoming impatience with mindfulness.

3. "Mindfulness-Based Stress Reduction (MBSR)" (Coursera/Udemy): Mindfulness techniques for managing stress and impatience.

4. "Mindfulness for Beginners" (Udemy): Practical mindfulness techniques for reducing impatience.

5. Mindful Schools: Mindfulness Courses: Developing patience, emotional regulation, and self-awareness.

Emotional Intelligence and Relationships

1. "Emotional Intelligence" (Coursera/Yale University): Understanding emotional intelligence, including patience and self-regulation.

2. "Emotional Intelligence: Master the Skills of a Super Communicator" (Udemy): Enhancing emotional intelligence for better patience and social interactions.

3. "Managing Difficult Conversations" (LinkedIn Learning): Effective communication for reducing impatience and conflict.

4. "Conflict Resolution: Finding Common Ground" (Coursera): Communication strategies for managing impatience and conflict.

Leadership and Patience

1. "The Power of Patience and Empathy in the Workplace" (LinkedIn Learning): Improving communication and relationships at work.

2. "Leading with Patience and Persistence" (LinkedIn Learning): Patience in leadership for better team management.

3. "Leadership Principles" (Harvard Business School Online): Balancing long-term patience with quick decision-making.

Personal Growth and Resilience

1. "Growth Mindset Masterclass" (Udemy): Developing a growth mindset and improving resilience.

2. "The Mindful Self-Compassion Program" (Online Course): Developing self-compassion and emotional resilience.

3. "Building Resilience and Patience" (Udemy): Tools for handling difficult situations with patience and resilience.

These online courses offer a range of topics and skills for cultivating patience, mindfulness, and emotional intelligence.

ACTIVITIES

WORKSHOPS AND RETREATS

1. Vipassana Meditation Retreats: 10-day silent retreats to deepen patience through meditation and self-observation.

2. Mindful Leadership Institute: Workshops for professionals to integrate mindfulness and improve patience under pressure.

3. The Art of Living's Happiness Program: A three-day residential course teaching breathing techniques and mindfulness practices to reduce stress and develop patience.

4. Tara Brach's Mindfulness Retreats: These in-person and virtual retreats focus on mindfulness and self-compassion to cultivate patience.

5. The Chopra Center's Meditation Retreats: These retreats focus on relaxation, self-compassion, and deep mindfulness practices to develop patience.

6. Omega Institute's Patience and the Path to Fulfilment Retreat: A retreat combining mindfulness and reflective exercises to build patience in daily life.

7. Mindfulness-Based Stress Reduction (MBSR) Retreats: These retreats teach mindfulness principles and applications to reduce impatience and stress.

8. The Mindful Self-Compassion (MSC) Programme: Workshops developing self-compassion and mindfulness.

9. Thich Nhat Hanh Retreats (Plum Village): These mindfulness retreats cultivate deep patience, compassion, and inner peace.

10. The Emotional Intelligence Retreat (Six Seconds): A retreat enhancing emotional intelligence, including patience-building exercises and empathy development.

11. The Insight Meditation Society (IMS): Meditation retreats cultivating mindfulness, patience, and self-awareness.

12. Esalen Institute: Mindfulness and Patience Workshops: These workshops combine mindfulness, yoga, and spiritual exploration to cultivate patience.

13. The Search Inside Yourself Leadership Institute: Workshops focusing on mindfulness, emotional intelligence, and leadership.

14. Mindful Leadership Retreat: These retreats teach mindful leadership, patience, acceptance, and navigating life's uncertainties.

APPS FOR MINDFULNESS AND PATIENCE

1. Headspace: Guided meditation and mindfulness exercises to develop patience and emotional resilience.

2. Calm: Mindfulness practices, sleep stories, and relaxation exercises to foster patience and reduce anxiety.

3. Insight Timer: Thousands of guided meditations to help users cultivate mindfulness and patience.

4. Forest: Gamifies focus and patience by allowing users to grow virtual trees as they stay focused.

5. MyLife Meditation (formerly Stop, Breathe & Think): Mood-based meditations to improve emotional awareness and patience.

6. Breathe: Guided meditations and breathing techniques to manage impatience and stress.

7. Smiling Mind: Programs for emotional awareness and stress management to reduce impatience.

ACTIVITIES

8. 10% Happier: Meditation and mindfulness practices to promote happiness and patience.

9. Moodfit: Mental health and self-improvement app to track mood, stress levels, and mindfulness exercises.

10. Pacifica: Cognitive-behavioural therapy techniques and mindfulness exercises to develop patience and emotional control.

These apps offer a range of tools and techniques to help users cultivate patience, mindfulness, and emotional resilience.

These workshops and retreats offer a range of opportunities for individuals to develop patience, mindfulness, and emotional intelligence in a supportive and immersive environment.

SELECTIVE READINGS

1. THE IMPATIENCE EPIDEMIC - *WHY WE STRUGGLE WITH PATIENCE*

We live in a world addicted to *instant gratification*. From social media to tech and fast-paced routines, life feels like it's always on fast-forward. This chapter dives into impatience—how it shows up in everyday annoyances like waiting in line or more profound struggles with emotional control. It introduces the *Impatience-to-Patience Continuum*, a tool that helps you understand the spectrum of impatience and patience. It's not a binary switch but a gradual shift from reactive to mindful. Simple mindfulness exercises show how small shifts can lead to significant changes. Recognising where you are on the continuum is the first step to consciously choosing *patience*.

2. THE IMPATIENT ME - *UNDERSTANDING MY TRIGGERS*

Impatience thrives on *triggers*—tight deadlines, unpredictable situations, or noisy environments. These stressors shape how we react, often dragging us into a spiral of anxiety and negative thinking. But impatience isn't set in stone. Reframing it as a chance to *pause and reflect* can help you regain control and think more clearly. In a fast-moving world, choosing patience isn't just a reaction; it's a strategy for better decisions and peace of mind.

How will you practise more patience—at work, with others, or in moments of self-care? The answer lies in those reflective pauses.

3. Why We Rush - *Unpacking the Roots*

Impatience often involves external pressures, personal habits, and early life experiences. For instance, the Crimean War disaster illustrates how impatience can cloud judgment and lead to disastrous consequences. Daily, impatience arises from waiting, unmet expectations, or external chaos. Recognising impatience triggers, such as perfectionism, FOMO, or chaotic environments, is crucial for managing them. By practising mindfulness, embracing self-compassion, and setting realistic expectations, we can shift our mindset and build patience. Understanding the causes of impatience allows us to transform frustration into personal growth and improved decision-making.

4. The Cost of Impatience - *How Frustration Affects My Life*

We explore how impatience affects our lives, from personal struggles to societal pressures. Modern dilemmas, like the rise of fast food, social media, and on-demand entertainment, fuel our need for instant gratification, leading to stress and poor decision-making. Real-world examples, such as the Samsung Galaxy Note 7 and Apple's MobileMe, demonstrate the high cost of impatience. The *Patience Pyramid* offers a solution, emphasising self-awareness, emotional regulation, and mindfulness to build patience over time. We can reclaim our calm, improve relationships, and make better decisions by embracing patience. Ultimately, patience offers long-term rewards, while impatience leads to short-term failures.

5. Social Factors - *A Patience Trap*

This chapter explored how social factors influence impatience in various aspects of life. *Rushing for results* in the workplace highlights how deadlines and quotas fuel impatience, leading to stress and mistakes, yet *patience* often results in better outcomes. *Relationship dynamics* are tested by impatience, where *communication* and *active listening* can prevent misunderstandings and foster understanding. *Impatience in everyday life*—whether in traffic, queues, or dealing with technology—reflects the societal *pressure* to hurry, but learning to slow down can lead to greater peace. Finally, the *Patience Toolbox* offers practical exercises, such as *empathy-building* and *assertive communication*, to build patience and improve social interactions across personal and professional lives.

6. MINDSET SHIFT - *REFRAMING OUR LENSES*

Shifting our *mindset* allows us to view challenges as opportunities for growth while adopting *mindfulness* and *self-compassion*, which helps us stay kind to ourselves and reduce *stress*. Changing our *perspective* on *time* encourages us to embrace the process, knowing that *small shifts* can lead to significant change. Reframing *patience* as an active skill helps us manage setbacks and remain resilient.

A *growth mindset* transforms how we react to obstacles, viewing them as steps towards success. The science behind *patience* shows that it improves *cognitive function*, reduces *stress*, and fosters emotional regulation.

7. A WORLD IN HURRY – *A NEW NORMAL*

This chapter explores the *erosion of patience* in modern society, driven by *technological acceleration* and a *culture shift* prioritising *instant gratification*. The rise of *social pressure* and the *cult of instant gratification* fuels impatience, while *psychological* and *societal impacts* such as *stress* and *anxiety* further shape our behaviours. The *neuroscience of impatience* reveals how the brain is rewired for quick rewards, diminishing our capacity for patience. The *manifestations of patience* in a *starved world* highlight the costs of constantly rushing, showing that while impatience leads to short-term results, it undermines long-term growth and well-being.

8. Accept What We Can't Control – *A Reflection*

This chapter highlights the importance of accepting what we can't control and balancing *macro patience* with *micro controls*. It discusses how we often try to control small things, but real growth comes from learning to manage *fixed structures* that limit us. The chapter encourages us to *embrace life's uncertainty*, recognising that things like time, mortality, and unexpected events require patience and acceptance. It also touches on *social dynamics*, stressing the need to accept others' choices and show understanding. We can build stronger relationships and foster personal growth by letting go of control. Ultimately, the chapter reminds us that patience is key to navigating an impatient world.

9. Leadership in an Impatient World

In an *impatient world*, leaders must recognise the *power of patience* as a critical leadership tool, enabling them to balance short-term pressures with long-term goals. Most successful leaders thrive by combining *steadiness* with *quick decision-making*, adapting when necessary while remaining focused on the bigger picture. Applying *Expectancy Theory* helps leaders align effort with expected rewards, fostering team motivation and trust. Leaders who are *consistently reliable* but *occasionally extraordinary* build trust through steady actions while delivering bold, impactful moments when the time is right. This blend of reliability and brilliance is essential for navigating the complexities of modern leadership.

10. Cultivating Patience

The chapter on Cultivating Patience covered how *meditation* and *mindfulness* can help calm your mind and build patience over time. The

SELECTIVE READINGS

5-Step Model for Cultivating Patience showed how to acknowledge, assess, adjust, act, and absorb emotions to stay patient. We also explored the role of *emotional intelligence* and *self-awareness* in recognising and managing our reactions. *Time management* and *prioritisation* techniques were covered to help you handle stress and stay focused on what matters. Ultimately, it's all about practising these skills to nurture patience in an impatient world.

AVAILABLE ON MOST ONLINE STORES

www.ingramcontent.com/pod-product-compliance
Lightning Source LLC
LaVergne TN
LVHW041704070526
838199LV00045B/1192